Houghton
Mifflin
Harcourt

On Our Way to English®

Student Edition

Printed in the U.S.A.

ISBN 978-0-544-23532-8

2 3 4 5 6 7 8 9 10   0868   22 21 20 19 18 17 16 15 14
4500461315   A B C D E F G

ON YOUR WAY

You're on your way to English. Soon you will listen, speak, read, and write English as if you had been doing it your whole life! This book will get you there, and so will your teacher.

Be yourself. Tell others what you think about what you are learning. Invite them to share their thoughts with you, too.

Sometimes your classmates will help you. Sometimes you'll help them. Even though you come from different places, you are all on the same journey.

Listening

The more English you hear, the more English you will understand. It won't all happen at once, but it will happen faster than you expect.

So, listen closely. If you don't understand, ask questions. That's an important part of learning.

Sometimes, your eyes will help you listen! Pictures will show you what's happening at the same time that you hear all about it.

Speaking

With this program, you'll learn and say new English words every day. You'll use them, too. You'll learn how to put the words together. Your English will get better and better.

Speaking English will help you in almost every part of your life. You'll be able to share information and ideas. You'll be able to express your own thoughts and opinions in English.

Reading

Most of the words you will
see in the United States are
written in English. You can see
words everywhere. They tell you the news. They
give you the information you need. They tell you
stories, and they tell you what people are like all
around the world. Without words, you'd miss
out on almost everything!

In this book, you will learn how to understand
simple ideas that are written down. Then you'll
start to understand written ideas that aren't so
simple. Keep going, and you'll get there.

Writing

You'll listen to English, speak it, and read it, too. As you do, you'll learn more words and more ways to put them together. At the same time, you'll be using what you learn to write in English.

You'll learn about different kinds of writing. You'll write your own letters, stories, and reports in English. Your teacher will show you how to start each writing project. Then you'll learn how to improve your work and make it really great!

GET GOING

The most important piece of the puzzle is you. You'll know when you're doing well and when you need help. It will be your job to push yourself ahead.

Keep going. You're on your way to English.

Contents

Faces and Places

The BIG Question

How are people and places in our world alike and different?

☐ What are some countries that people come from?

☐ How are foods in this country different from foods in some other places?

☐ What sports do people from many places like to play?

1. **What holidays or celebrations do you know about?**

   I know about…
   - ☐ Thanksgiving.
   - ☐ Presidents' Day.
   - ☐ the Fourth of July.
   - ☐ birthdays.

2. **What is your homeland like?**

   My homeland has…
   - ☐ hills.
   - ☐ the sea.
   - ☐ flat land.
   - ☐ a big river.

3. What symbols do we share?

We share...

☐

☐

☐

☐

4. What can you find on some maps?

On some maps, I can find...

☐ a compass rose.

☐ the population of our state.

☐ a scale of miles.

☐ the name of this country.

Say **more!**

Learn the Words

affect

symbol

trail

celebrate

scale

market

Theme Vocabulary

The easiest way to remember the meaning of a new word is to use the word. As you discuss people and places, use these vocabulary words. Use them when you read and write about people and places, too.

Read the word.

Look at the picture.

Listen to your teacher.

affect

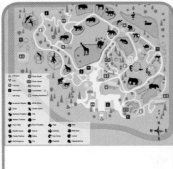

symbol

trail

celebrate

scale

market

Which Picture?

Look at the vocabulary cards. Choose one picture.
Don't tell anyone what it is! Describe the picture.
See if your partner can guess which picture you chose.

MUDDY SHOES

 Sylvia **Mom**

Mom got a new rug. It is shaggy and white.

①

Muddy shoes are bad for white rugs…

②

… so I take my shoes off when I come home.

③

But today, something is wrong.

④

Oh no!

⑤

There is mud on Mom's rug!

I did not get mud on the rug. But I know who did.

6

Mud is stubborn. It is hard to clean up.

RUB
RUB

7

Mom is going to flip her lid.

RUB RUB RUB RUB RUB RUB

8

Sylvia! Why is there mud on my rug?

9

Did you wear your muddy shoes in the house?

10

8 Formal/Informal Language Saying that someone will "flip her lid" is an informal way to say that she will be very upset or angry. You use the expression only in informal situations.

13

12 **Formal/Informal Language** When Sylvia's mother says to her, "You have disappointed me," she is using formal language. How could you say this expression in an informal way? When could you use an informal expression?

I know that I should not have lied.

But I could not tell on Bo.

Bo is my friend. So I will take the blame for him.

WAG WAG WAG

 16 Expressions To "tell on" someone is an informal expression that means to tell somebody else that the person has done something he or she should not have done.

G⊙ West!

Come out to the coast of California and Oregon. There's an adventure waiting for you!

WALK AMONG GIANTS

Take a walk through Redwoods National Park in northern California. A few redwoods here are 2,000 years old! They're the oldest living things on Earth. Redwoods are the tallest trees, too. Some grow to be 370 feet tall.

WATCH FOR WHALES

California gray whales migrate from Alaska to Mexico and back again. Point Reyes Peninsula may be the best place on the **continent** to watch them. One of the whales' "highways" lies close by.

EXPLORE ASTORIA

Astoria, Oregon, began as a **market** for fur traders. It was a major **fishing** port, too. Shipwrecks lie in the waters around Astoria. They are a **symbol** of the city's stormy seagoing past.

HIKE HOOD

Mount Hood is Oregon's tallest mountain. It is a volcano, but that shouldn't **affect** you. The peak hasn't erupted for many years. Some of Mount Hood is covered with snow year-round.

17

Camping with the Bears

by Dina Baker

I was trapped in a tent with my little brother. Sam was asleep, but I poked him until he woke up. When I asked where Mom and Dad were, Sam said they were with the bears.

Now I was really scared. Sam and I were in a cheap little tent in the Sierra National Forest, home to many black bears. And our parents were missing!

It was all up to me, so I took action.

First, I turned the volume way up on Dad's radio. Second, I made Sam lie face down and play dead. I did, too. That way, we wouldn't seem so scary to the bears.

We needed even more noise. So Sam and I started singing EEE-I-EEE-I-O at the top of our lungs. We kept this up for thirty minutes!

And that was how our parents found us. By then, I was even more upset. Mom gave me a pat and said they were just helping a nice young couple, the Bairds.

"The bears?" I asked. "As in *Grrr*?"

Mom laughed. "Of course not! We said The *Bairds*—not the *bears*. They didn't know how to set up their tent."

Then she added with a big smile, "They must not be from around here. All of us know how to camp!"

HOW TO PREVENT A BROWN BEAR ATTACK

Step 1: Make noise
Step 2: Play dead
Step 3: Act human
(Bears care about their cubs, just as we do.)

19

The Oregon Trail

by Alex Mazenko

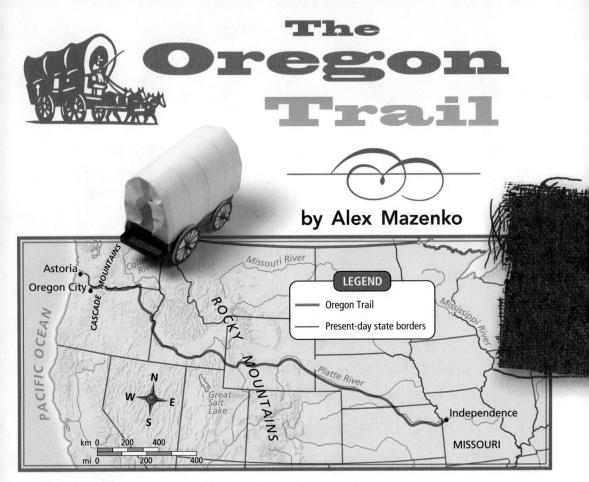

During the 1830s and 1840s, most of America's **population** lived in the East. In the Far West, Oregon had rich land for **farming** and rivers for fishing. How could people get to this land?

The Oregon Trail was the most **common** way. More than 300,000 Americans traveled this route. The **trail** stretched from the Mississippi River to central Oregon. From the **scale** on the map, you can see that is about 2,000 miles (3,200 km).

The trip along the trail took about five months.
Travelers usually rode in covered wagons. They
packed everything they needed. Sturdy oxen pulled
the heavy loads.

How did the trip affect people? Families faced
freezing cold and burning heat. Sometimes they ran
out of food and water.

Countless wagons
crossed the Oregon Trail.
Ruts left by their wheels
can still be seen today.
Those ruts are a symbol
of a great movement west.

Prove It

What are some
problems that travelers
faced on the Oregon
Trail? Where do you
learn about these
problems?

A Perfect Day?

by Duncan Searl

The sun was shining. The ocean was bright blue. The Ruiz family's sailboat flew over the waves. "What a perfect day!" said Mr. Ruiz to his daughters.

Actually, the day hadn't been perfect. Kim and Dawn Ruiz didn't say anything, though. Their father had said they would see some whales. A large population of California gray whales was in the area. But so far they hadn't seen a single one.

"Yes, a perfect day," Mr. Ruiz repeated. Unfortunately, he spoke too soon.

With a loud thump, the sailboat suddenly hit a sandbar. Mr. Ruiz frowned. He got out a map. He checked the scale of miles and the **compass rose**. He found the symbol for sandbars. "There shouldn't be any sandbars near here!" he said. "Now we're stuck!" The sailboat was on the sand and couldn't move.

Six-year-old Kim began to cry. "Are we shipwrecked?"

Twelve-year-old Dawn comforted her sister. "No, we're just stuck. We'll get off this sandbar." She looked over at their father. "Right?"

"With the ocean's help, we will," said Mr. Ruiz. "We'll have to wait for high tide, though."

"What's high tide?" asked Kim.

Zoom In

What details tell you that this story is set on the sea? Check the words and the pictures.

Dawn tried to explain. "The moon affects the level of the sea," she began. "The water rises and falls each day due to the moon's gravitational pull."

Kim didn't understand. "So we're waiting for the moon to pull us off?" she finally asked.

"You could say that," replied Dawn. "And it could be a long wait."

Mr. Ruiz got out the fishing rods, but nobody caught anything. The girls ate the last two apples they had gotten at the market that morning. "Getting stuck on sandbars is a common problem," Mr. Ruiz said. That didn't make anyone feel better.

Dawn and Kim kept their eyes on the sandbar. At 4 P.M., the water started to rise. By 6 P.M., water almost covered the sandbar. Would it rise high enough?

Suddenly, a gray whale and her calf leaped into the air just past the sandbar. "Whales!" the girls shouted. Seconds later the whales were gone. Only a trail of bubbles remained behind.

The splash from the whales did it! The sailboat slid off the sandbar with a slurp. Mr. Ruiz and the girls began to **celebrate**. Half an hour later, they were home.

"What a day," said Mr. Ruiz.

"What a perfect ending to a day," said Dawn.

Prove It

What is the family's problem? How is it solved? Tell where you find out in the story.

Hello!

Pedro

Hello! My name is Pedro. I am from São Paulo, Brazil. The population of Sao Paulo is over 10 million people. It's one of the ten largest cities in the world.

My family moved to Los Angeles, California. At first, I didn't speak any English at all. A lot of people in California are from Latin America. They spoke to me in Spanish. I didn't understand that, either! In Brazil, people speak Portuguese, not Spanish.

São Paulo

It didn't take me long to understand Spanish, but English was more difficult. The kids in my classroom tried to help. Some spoke very slowly to me. Others spoke very loudly. There was only one problem. Slow or loud, I didn't know what the words meant.

Little by little, I learned more English. At home, I studied my dictionary. I looked up common English words. Then I practiced saying them.

My teacher also asked me to speak English to her. She said to try! She also told me to listen. Soon, her work began to affect me.

I started learning faster and faster. Now, as you can see, I am good at English! And when friends speak to me, I know what to say back to them.

Zoom In

How is Pedro like other newcomers in Los Angeles? How is he different?

Wen

Hello! My name is Wen. I was born in Beijing, the capital of China. When I was young, I loved going to the market with my mother. There is a lot of farming and fishing in China, so there is a lot of fresh food.

Two years ago, my family decided to move to California. I was so afraid. I thought my whole life would change completely.

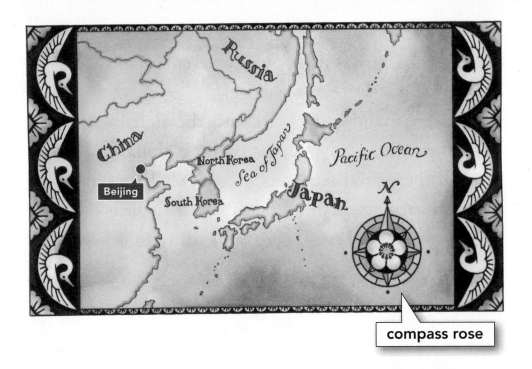

compass rose

Well, my life has changed, but not completely. For example, I loved playing Chinese jump rope back in China. So now I've taught the game to my new friends here.

I thought that I would be the only Chinese girl in Los Angeles, but I'm not. I've also made friends from all over the world.

There's also plenty of fresh food here in California. Chinese markets are common. There are dozens of Chinese restaurants too. Even so, I still prefer my mother's cooking!

At home my family still speaks Mandarin, the same as in China. At school, however, I had to speak English. That was a big change!

To learn English, I began with the alphabet. Did you know Chinese languages have no alphabet? Instead there are thousands of symbols that stand for words. Learning them all takes years. English only has twenty-six letters. That's something to celebrate!

Beijing

English has more vowel sounds than Chinese. Sometimes I get them wrong. I'm not used to hearing the different sounds. When I listen harder, it helps a lot.

Today I try to speak English as much as I can. Sure, I'll make some mistakes. But that's okay. Sometimes, making mistakes is a good way to learn.

To practice English, I sometimes repeat what other people have said. That causes problems, though. In one class, a girl told me, "I've spoken English my whole life." So I replied, "I've spoken English my whole life since last summer." Everybody laughed, and I didn't know why. Now I can enjoy the joke too.

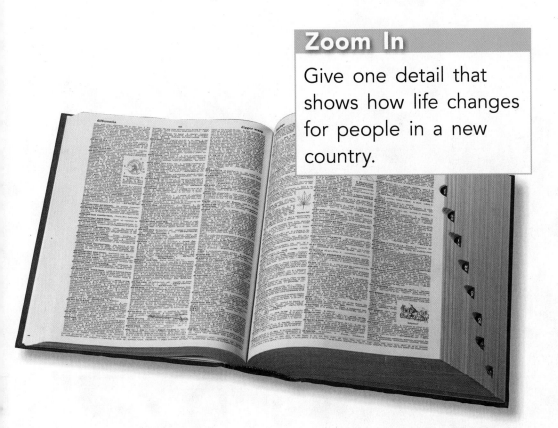

Zoom In

Give one detail that shows how life changes for people in a new country.

Fernando

Hello! My name is Fernando. I am from Lima, the capital of Peru. Peru is on the continent of South America. Today, I live in Los Angeles, California.

Lima is on the Pacific Ocean. So is Los Angeles. Lima has warm sunny summers and mild winters. So does Los Angeles. So I feel right at home in California.

Los Angeles

In Lima, I spoke two languages. One was Quechua. Millions of people around the Andes Mountains speak this language. It's mainly a spoken language, though. Not many books are printed in Quechua.

I also spoke Spanish. At school, most of our classes were in Spanish. Our books were printed in Spanish, too.

compass rose

In Los Angeles, many people speak Spanish. So that feels like home. Not many speak Quechua, though.

Now I'm learning English in school. So I'll be able to speak two languages here, too—English and Spanish.

Cusco

▲ The Festival of the Sun

Last winter, we were still in Peru. My parents took me to Cusco, a city high in the Andes. We went there for the Festival of the Sun. It is held once a year, on the day with the least sunlight. This festival is a lot of fun to celebrate!

I'm sure I'll find a lot of new holidays to celebrate in my new country, too.

Prove It

How many children tell their stories? What evidence did you use to find out?

MACHU PICCHU

by J.J. Elmhurst

Most visitors to Peru want to see Machu Picchu. This city was built by the Incas over 500 years ago. From the city of Cusco, a trail stretches fifty miles up into the Andes Mountains to Machu Picchu. Machu Picchu stands on a mountain 8,000 feet above sea level.

Some visitors walk the steep trail up to Machu Picchu. The hike takes about four days. Most travelers take a train from Cusco.

Machu Picchu has almost 200 buildings. Stone palaces and temples are in one part of the city. There are plazas and large houses too. Smaller houses and fields for farming are in another area.

The Incas were amazing builders. They had no steel or iron tools. Yet they cut giant blocks of stone. The Incas had no cement to hold stones together. So every stone had to fit perfectly.

The Incas had no wagons or work animals. Even so, they moved giant building stones up the mountain.

Work on Machu Picchu began around 1450. Nobody is sure why the city was built. There are some explanations though.

Machu Picchu may have been a palace for Inca kings. It may have been a center of religion. It may have been a fort. It may have been a place to study the stars. Perhaps it was all those things.

About 1,000 people lived in and around Machu Picchu. The population didn't stay very long. By 1572, the Incas had left the city for good. They may have been affected by diseases brought by Spanish explorers.

▲ The llama is a symbol of Peru.

The Spanish had conquered the Incas by 1542. They never found out about Machu Picchu. The mountaintop city was just one small spot on a huge continent.

As time passed, people forgot about Machu Picchu. Steep cliffs made the city hard to reach. Vines and plants hid the buildings. A great Inca city had all but disappeared.

Zoom In

What details show why people forgot about Machu Picchu as time went on?

▲ The Incas changed the sides of the hills so they could farm there.

Hiram Bingham, an American explorer, searched the Andes for many years. In 1911, he had something to celebrate. A small boy led Bingham to the ruins of Machu Picchu. The explorer called it "the lost city of the Incas."

Bingham and his team studied the site carefully. Just clearing away the vines took years. The explorers tried to learn as much as possible.

The Incas had no written language. They left no records of why they built the city or why they left it. In many ways, Machu Picchu remains a puzzle.

▲ an example of Incan building skill

Machu Picchu is no longer a lost city. In fact, it's the most famous place in Peru. Many travelers visit every year.

All those visitors are hard on the site and the surrounding land. Today, the government of Peru protects Machu Picchu so that the city will always remain a symbol of Peru's Inca past.

Prove It

Why was Machu Picchu called a "lost city"? How do you know?

Learn the Words

farming
fishing
population
continent
compass rose
common

- Read the words on the list.
- Read the dialogue.
- Find the words.

This sign should really have a **compass rose**. I can't tell if we're looking north, south, east, or west.

This place has a **population** of about 50,000 people.

Many of them make their living by **farming**.

1. Write a Travel Ad
Writing

Write an ad about the place in the picture. Tell why people should visit there. You can make up things that aren't shown in the picture. Use "Go West!" in this unit as a model. Show your idea to a partner.

2. Make a Chart
Graphic Organizer

Which other continents have your classmates lived on? Ask several classmates. Tally their responses. Share your findings with your partner.

Continent	How Many Lived There?
South America	
Europe	
Asia	
Africa	

3. Use a Compass Rose
Listening and Speaking

How do you use a compass rose to find north, south, east, and west on a map? If a compass rose labels only the north, how do you find south, east, and west? Work with a partner. Come up with at least three steps. Share your how-to with your partner.

4. Make a List
Vocabulary

How many foods can you name that come from a farm? Think of things that grow and things that come from animals. Make a list. See how many farm foods you can name.

Foods from a Farm

Chinese Jump Rope

by Claudia Chang

This game is over 1,000 years old. It's usually played with two enders and one jumper.

1. You need an elastic rope about 15 feet long. You can make one with rubber bands. Tie the ends together so you have a big loop.

2. The two enders stand facing each other, with the loop around their ankles. They move back until the rope is stretched.

ankle

3. Agree on the rules for your jumps.
   Here's a common pattern:
   + Jump so both feet land inside the rope.
   + Jump so one foot is outside, on the right.
   + Jump so one foot is outside, on the left.
   + Jump so both feet are outside the rope.
   + Jump so both feet land on the rope.
4. Your turn is over if you make a mistake. If you
   don't, the rope gets moved up the legs of the
   enders. If it gets too high, start a new pattern.
5. What are you waiting for? Start jumping!

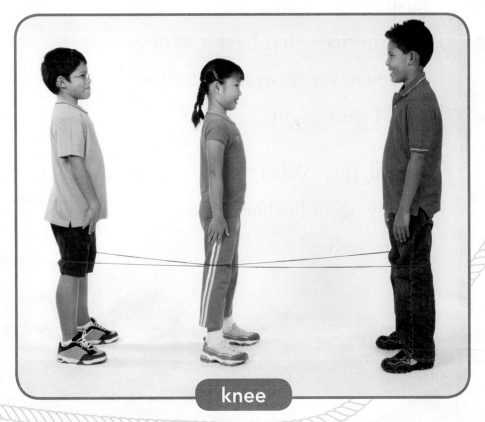

knee

Oranges

by Alejo Cruz

All I wanted was a carton of juice.
But I got mixed up and asked
For a crate of oranges.

Learning a new language isn't easy.
People notice when I get it wrong.
But they never seem to be around
When I get it right.

They ask me, "Where do you come from?"
But they never bother to ask,
"Where are you going?"

Retell "Hello!"

 When you retell a selection, tell only the main ideas and details. This helps readers understand the selection.

"Hello!" is a personal narrative. Three Los Angeles children tell about their homelands. Review the selection on pages 26–35. Look at the chart on page 49.

■ Top Row: Who is the first child? Where did he come from? Where does he live now? What is an important fact about his homeland?

■ Middle Row: Who is the second child? Where did she come from? Where does she live now? What is an important fact about her homeland?

■ Bottom Row: Who is the third child? Where did he come from? Where does he live now? What is an important fact about his homeland?

Use the chart on page 49 to retell the selection to your partner. As you tell about each child, point to the correct pictures. Use complete sentences.

Words you might use in your retelling:	
market	continent
farming	fishing

São Paulo,
Brazil

Pedro

Wen

Los Angeles,
U.S.A.

Beijing,
China

Lima,
Peru

Fernando

Dig Deeper

Look Back

The main idea of a text is its most important idea. You read about Machu Picchu. Think about an ad you could make to get people to visit this place. Your ad should show the most important idea about Machu Picchu in the biggest print.

Work with a partner. Look back at "Machu Picchu." What detail about Machu Picchu would you put in the biggest print in your ad?

Talk About It

Which child in the selection "Hello!" gives the most useful or interesting information about his or her country?

Why do you think so?

Do you agree with your classmates? Why or why not?

If not, how could you convince others to change their minds? How could others convince you to change your mind?

Conversation

> **i** When you have a conversation, you talk. You also listen. You listen to the information your friend gives you. You listen to what your friend is asking you.

Talk to a partner. One of you will be person A. The other will be person B.

Person A

Person B

Say hello and ask your partner's name.

Reply. Ask your partner's name.

Answer. Ask where your partner's family comes from.

Reply. Ask your partner the same question.

Reply. Say goodbye.

Say goodbye.

Crafty Creatures

The **BIG** Question

How do animals meet their needs?

- ☐ How can animals use their sense of smell?
- ☐ Can animals use tools?
- ☐ How do animals know where they are going?

1. What things are a part of nature?

Some things from nature are...

☐ plants.

☐ animals.

☐ seas, lakes, and rivers.

☐ clouds and rain.

2. What mammals do you know?

I know about...

☐ cats.

☐ dogs.

☐ monkeys.

☐ elephants.

3. How can you describe a bird?

A bird has...

☐ feathers.

☐ a bill.

☐ wings.

☐ just two feet.

4. What can some animals do?

Some animals can...

☐ build a nest.

☐ spin a web.

☐ dig a hole.

☐ use sticks or stones as tools.

Say **more!**

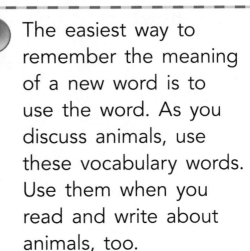

Learn the Words

unique
trait
nature
fish
fin
scales

Theme Vocabulary

The easiest way to remember the meaning of a new word is to use the word. As you discuss animals, use these vocabulary words. Use them when you read and write about animals, too.

Read the word.

Look at the picture.

Listen to your teacher.

unique

trait

nature

fish

fin

scales

Match the Pictures

Look at the pictures on the vocabulary cards. Choose two pictures that go together. Tell why you think the pictures go together.

57

LUKE'S BAD DAY

 Luke   Mom

Saturday was a bad day for Luke. He woke up late.

Oh no!

1

He broke his bike.

2

He missed his bus.

Where is Luke?

3

He was late for his game.

Luke sure is late!

4

Strike three!

He struck out twice.

5

6 Luke was down in the dumps.

7 He found a bug on his big red rug.

8 I'm going to squash that bug!

Luke's mom had a piece of advice.

9 If you let the bug go, it will bring good luck.

10 Luke wasn't sure…

11 …but he gave it a try.

6 Formal/Informal Language When someone is "down in the dumps," the person is very unhappy. Is this expression formal language or informal language?

59

The next day, things started to turn around.

SUNDAY

3

12

Luke woke up on time.

06:30

13

14

He fixed his busted bike.

15

He made the bus.

 14 **Formal/Informal Language** The word *busted* is slang. It means "broken." Would you ever use this word when talking to your principal? Why, or why not?

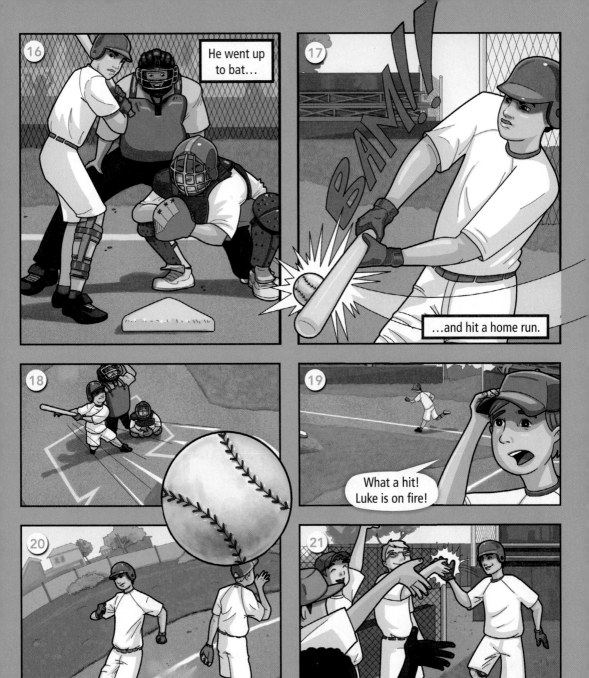

16 He went up to bat…

17 …and hit a home run.

18

19 What a hit! Luke is on fire!

20 He ran the bases, all the way to home.

21 Sunday was a good day for Luke.

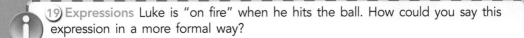

19 **Expressions** Luke is "on fire" when he hits the ball. How could you say this expression in a more formal way?

ANIMALS USING TOOLS

by Naomi Tyler

People used to say, "Humans are **unique**. They are the only animals that use tools." They were wrong! Some **mammals** and **birds** in **nature** use tools, too.

On Land

Elephants often tear branches from trees. They use the branches to swat flies. They often drop rocks onto the electric fence around a field to crush the fence. That **causes** the electricity to cut off. Then the elephants walk safely into the field to find food.

Sometimes a gorilla uses a stick to see how deep water is. If it's not too deep, the gorilla wades in, using the stick as a cane.

At Sea

Bottle-nosed dolphins have a strange **trait**. They search the seabed for sponges. When a dolphin finds one the right size, it wears it on its beak! The sponge protects the beak from scratches and poisonous sea animals.

Sea otters like to eat abalone. These sea animals live in shells, though. So otters carry stones with them as they dive. They hammer at the abalone shells to get them off the rocks.

In the Air

Some birds use twigs to dig for insects. Crows are very smart birds. One crow couldn't reach some food with its **bill**. So the crow bent a piece of wire to make a hook! This tool helped the crow get a meal.

Report

Never Call a Spider an Insect

by Kevin Waddy

Spiders and insects are alike in some ways. Both have hard outer skeletons. Both have eyes and legs. Many people call both of them "bugs."

Spiders are not insects. They are arachnids, so they have eight legs. A spider's body is divided into two parts called the cephalothorax and the abdomen. Spiders have eight eyes. They smell through bristles on their legs.

Spiders eat mostly insects, but they also eat small frogs and mice. Most spiders make webs and produce silk.

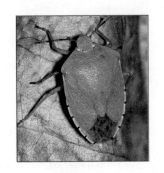

Insects are not arachnids. Insects have three body parts called the head, the thorax, and the abdomen. Unlike arachnids, insects have two antennae that help them smell. They have just two eyes. Many insects have wings. Insects eat almost anything, including paper, plastic, and lint.

How to Build a
TRAP

by T. Rodriguez

A spider web is a unique trap. Nothing else in nature is quite like it. Spiders spin webs to catch insects. Not all spiders can spin webs, but many do have this skill.

A spider web stretches between two objects. They may be the branches of a bush, or even the legs of a chair. The material for the web is called silk. It comes from inside the spider's body.

To begin the web, the spider spins a long thin thread. The thread makes a line between the two objects.

Next, the spider spins threads out from the first line. You could describe these threads as looking like the spokes of a bicycle wheel. Finally, the spider spins sticky threads in circles.

Once the web is finished, the spider waits. A spider doesn't wait on the web, though. A bird or reptile might see it there and eat it. So spiders hide near their webs.

At last an insect lands on the web. The sticky threads cause it to get stuck. The spider rushes up! It bites! It wraps the insect with more thread.

Dinner is served.

Prove It

What does the spider's web help the spider do? What part of the selection tells you?

Why Bear Sleeps So Much

based on a folktale

Cast of Characters

NARRATOR   BIRD   FISH   RABBIT   DEER
SQUIRREL   SNAKE   RACCOON   EAGLE

Setting: In the forest, next to a lake (where **FISH** *stays)*

NARRATOR: Today Bear sleeps through most of the winter. It's one of his best-known traits. It wasn't always that way, though. Bear used to stay awake year-round, day and night. That caused big problems for the other animals in nature. Once they even had a meeting to see what they could do about it.

BIRD: (*nervously*) Something has to be done about

Bear. He's always crashing into my tree and smashing my nest and eggs.

FISH: (*angrily*) He grabs me by the **fins** and **scales**. I'm afraid to swim anywhere these days.

RABBIT: And his big feet keep crushing my burrows. It isn't safe being underground.

DEER: (*gently*) Why don't we just ask Bear to be kinder and more thoughtful?

SQUIRREL: (*sneering at* DEER) Ha! That will never work. I would describe Bear as a bully. He really enjoys walking all over the rest of us.

SNAKE: Right! Bear stepped on my tail just last weekend. He can be very hard on a reptile.

SQUIRREL: Let's throw Bear in jail then! That'll fix him! He won't be able to hurt us then.

RACCOON: (*rubbing his paws together*) Great idea, Squirrel!

RABBIT: But friends, we don't have a jail. We'd have to build one. And then one of us would have to go into Bear's cell to feed him.

NARRATOR: The animals were silent. The thought of feeding Bear was too scary for words.

BIRD: (*sadly*) I guess there's nothing we can do.

SQUIRREL: Guess not.

SNAKE: I was afraid this would happen.

(*The disappointed animals turn away to head home. Suddenly, lightning flashes and thunder rolls. EAGLE enters.*)

EAGLE: (*loudly*) I just heard about the meeting, and I wanted to share an idea.

SQUIRREL: Let's hear it, Boss.

EAGLE: Bear wouldn't be able to hurt anyone if he was asleep. So let's pass a law that says he has to sleep for several months each winter. He'll have lots less time to cause trouble then.

RABBIT: I vote yes!

NARRATOR: In the end, all the animals voted yes. Bear would have to sleep in the winter months every year. It was the law. Surprisingly, Bear went along with the new law. He even liked it. For Bear had been overtired for years. That's why he caused so much trouble. Once Bear started getting enough sleep, he was much happier and easier to live with.

Prove It

Which animal solved the problem? How do you know?

How Do ANIMALS KNOW WHERE They Are GOING?

by Daud Ali

Animals don't all stay in one place for their whole lives. In fact, some animals travel very long distances. Many animals migrate from one place to another when the seasons change. Many move around to locate food or water. Some travel to find the best place to lay their eggs or give birth to their young.

Think how hard it is for people to find their way around. They have to ask directions. They need to look at a road map. Now, there is even GPS, but people still get lost all the time. Yet somehow elephants, small birds, salmon, and even bees always seem to get to where they need to go. How do they find their way around? It depends on the animal.

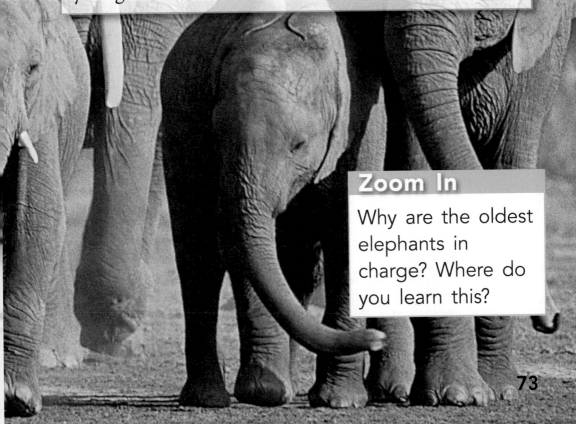

Landmarks

Many animals have good memories. If they have made a journey once, they will remember the way. That's because they recognize the landmarks. A landmark is anything that stands out in nature. Big trees, rocks, and ponds are all landmarks.

Elephants remember the way to many places. When the food is gone in one area, they travel to other feeding places. During the dry season, they go to certain places to dig for water. Elephants use landmarks to find these places.

The oldest elephants are always in charge. They remember the landmarks in more places than the younger ones do.

Zoom In

Why are the oldest elephants in charge? Where do you learn this?

Scent

Many mammals, birds, reptiles, and fish have a good sense of smell. They rely on this trait in many ways. They use scent to find food, to recognize friends and enemies, and to know where they are.

A salmon uses its fins to swim hundreds of miles up from the sea. Each salmon goes to the stream where it was born. To find the exact place, a salmon uses scent.

Bees also find places by scent. Each beehive has a unique smell. After a long flight, a bee uses scent to find it.

Zoom In

How does a bee find its own hive after a long flight? What evidence did you use for your answer?

The Sun

Some animals use the Sun to find the right direction in their travels. This sounds easy, but what if it's cloudy? Also, the position of the Sun in the sky changes during the day and during the year.

Many ants are experts at using the Sun. Sometimes they travel far from their nests. Scientists describe ants as having a "clock" in their bodies. This clock causes them to keep track of the Sun's position. So they travel home in a straight line and don't get lost.

Many birds use the Sun, too. They use the Sun to guide them on trips to feeding places. The Sun helps them when they migrate, too.

The Stars

Some animals travel at night. Most songbirds, for example, fly in the dark when they migrate.

Birds can't use the sun at night, but they still depend on the sky. They use the patterns of the stars as a guide.

The indigo bunting picks the North Star as its guide. It recognizes the star by its place in the pattern. The North Star doesn't change its position in the sky during the night.

The Moon isn't much help to night-flying birds. In fact, it gets in the way. When the Moon is bright, birds have a harder time seeing the stars.

Magnetism

If you hike through nature, you can use a compass to find the right way. Some animals have their own built-in compasses.

Baby loggerhead turtles find their way 8,000 miles across the ocean. They use Earth's magnetism. These reptiles know where they are and where they need to go.

Homing pigeons always fly home. That's how they got their name. On sunny days, they use the Sun. When it's cloudy, they use Earth's magnetism. One scientist used magnets to change the magnetism around some homing pigeons. The birds couldn't find their homes.

Prove It

What can you conclude about how the sky helps some animals find their way? What evidence did you use?

Loggerhead
Homecoming

by Angela Castillo

Loggerheads are one of the largest sea turtles. Most weigh about 250 pounds, but a few reach 1,000 pounds or more! Their shells, about three feet long, are reddish brown. The reptiles are named for their heavy, loglike heads.

Loggerheads eat jellyfish, crabs, and fish. Seaweed is on the menu, too.

Each summer, thousands of female loggerheads visit the beaches of Florida, Georgia, and South Carolina. The females dig nests in the sand and lay their eggs. Then they quickly return to the sea.

Once the eggs hatch, the two-inch babies scurry down the sand and into the water, too. The trip is short but dangerous. Raccoons, dogs, and gulls all prey on the tiny reptiles.

When they reach the water, the baby turtles swim out to sea. The dangers continue, though. Sea birds, fish, and ocean mammals feed on the turtles. Sometimes the turtles are trapped in the nets of fishing ships.

Meanwhile ocean currents sweep the young turtles far from their birthplaces. Many reach the middle of the Atlantic or the coasts of other continents.

Zoom In

Where do the baby turtles go after they hatch? How do you know?

The years pass, and the turtles grow. After about 20 years, the females are ready to go ashore and lay their own eggs for the first time.

Not any beach will do, though. The female loggerheads return home. That is, they lay their eggs at or near the beach where they themselves hatched. For thousands of turtles, that means swimming across the ocean.

For a long time, the turtles' homecoming was a mystery of nature. There are no landmarks to follow in the deep ocean. The turtles' eyes are made for seeing underwater. They can't really see the Sun or stars. Their sense of smell is not a trait they can count on. So how do loggerheads find their birthplace?

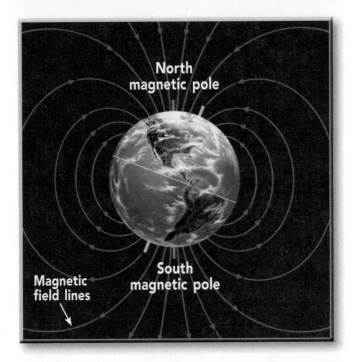

North
magnetic pole

South
magnetic pole

Magnetic
field lines

To answer that question, you need to know that
Earth is like a giant magnet.

The north pole of the magnet is near the top of
the planet. The south pole is near the bottom.
Magnetic field lines extend from these poles across
Earth and into space.

Loggerhead turtles are able to "read" Earth's
magnetic field. It's like having a GPS in your brain.

When each turtle hatches, the magnetic field of its
birthplace is set in its brain. So no matter where it
goes, the turtle can find its way back there.

Prove It

What makes turtles able to find
their way to their birthplace?
What evidence did you use?

Honey Badgers

by Michelle Liang

Its name sounds cute, but don't let that fool you. A honey badger is one of the toughest mammals in East Africa, even though it isn't much bigger than a house cat.

Using its long, strong claws, the honey badger is a fierce hunter. It can kill and eat a five-foot cobra in fifteen minutes, scales and all. Some honey badgers even scare away lions and steal their food!

A honey badger eats just about anything—small mammals, reptiles, fish, birds, fruit, roots. Its favorite food, however, is—you guessed it—honey.

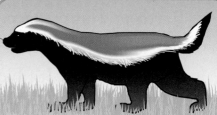

Length: 22–30 inches (not counting tail)
Tail: 5–12 inches
Height (at shoulders): 9–11 inches
Weight: 20–30 pounds

In East Africa, beehives are built high in trees.
The short-legged honey badger can't always see them.
So how does it get its favorite food?

Honey badgers are as clever as they are tough.
They use a bird to guide them to the beehives. Not
surprisingly, the bird is called a honeyguide.

Honeyguides eat insects, spiders, and fruit. What
honeyguides really love, though, is beeswax. That's
the wax that bees store their honey in.

A high-flying honeyguide can find a beehive, but it can't get the wax from it alone. The hive is deep inside the tree. Only a climbing mammal with sharp claws can dig out the honey and wax.

Down on the ground, the honey badger sees the honeyguide. The badger waits and watches. Near one tree, the bird makes a signal with its wings. Beehive!

The honey badger races to the tree and climbs up. Near the top, bees are buzzing in and out of a hole in the tree trunk. The honey badger goes to work. With its long claws, it tears away the bark and wood around the hive.

Once the hole is big enough, the badger begins to eat. It slurps up every drop of honey in the hive. The honey badger doesn't like wax though. So it leaves that behind.

After the badger leaves, it's the honeyguide's turn. The bird flies in and eats the wax in the hive. It also eats the insects that live in and around most beehives.

Both the badger and bird get a great meal. By working together, they help each other survive.

Zoom In

Which animal can find the beehives? What part of the selection tells you?

Sometimes the honeyguide hears a loud whistling sound. The bird knows just what it means. The Boran people of East Africa are looking for honey. They use a special whistle to call the honeyguide. They want the bird to help them, just as it helped the badger.

At the sound of the whistle, the honey badger hurries away. The Boran don't like honey badgers. That's because the badgers sometimes kill the people's chickens or steal their food supplies.

The honeyguide and the Boran work together, though. The bird flies over to the people. Then it looks for another tree with a beehive. The Boran keep their eyes on the bird until they see its signal.

When the bird signals, the Boran hurry over to the tree. One man with an ax and a pot climbs up. He opens up the beehive and scoops out the honey. Like the badger, the man leaves the wax behind.

Now the honeyguide goes in for another meal. There is more wax and insects than it can eat. So other honeyguides show up and share the feast.

By working with people—and honey badgers—the birds get plenty to eat. It's just another way that animals in nature cooperate.

Prove It

What is one way animals in this selection work together? Where did you find your evidence?

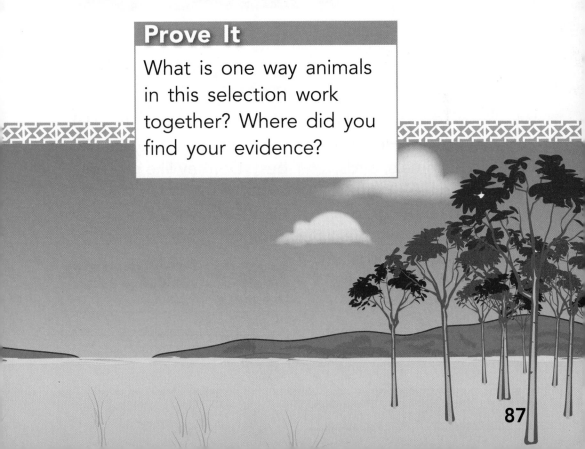

Learn the Words

bird

bill

cause

describe

mammal

reptile

- Read the words on the list.
- Read the dialogue.
- Find the words.

A lot of people came to help us.

The river cleanup is going well.

I just saw a **bird**. I don't know what kind it was, though.

You can tell by the feathers.

Or you can look at the shape of the **bill**.

1. Write a Play
Writing

Why must we keep the land and water clean? How does this help mammals, birds, reptiles, and fish? Work with your partner. Write a short play. Two people from the picture should be characters in the play. Use the play "Why Bear Sleeps So Much," in this unit, as a model.

2. Take a Survey
Graphic Organizer

Ask some classmates which type of animal they like best. Do they like reptiles, birds, or mammals? Tally their responses. Share your findings with a partner.

Your Favorite Kind of Animal	
mammals	
birds	
reptiles	

3. Plan a TV Show
Writing

Suppose you could plan a TV show about amazing animal skills. Write the first part of a script. It will have words for a TV announcer to say about one amazing animal. In your script, tell what the animal can do. Make the skill sound exciting. Show your script to your partner.

4. Describe It
Listening and Speaking

Describe a mammal, bird, or reptile. Tell your partner how it looks. Tell if it lives on land or in water. Also, listen as your partner describes an animal. Ask your partner questions about any words you don't understand.

The Crow and the Pitcher

retold by Kyla Roberts

Crow was thirsty, very thirsty. He had flown for miles, but he couldn't find water anywhere. At last, Crow spotted a pitcher on a table in someone's yard. Crow flew down to take a look. The pitcher was half-full of water.

The thirsty bird pushed his bill into the pitcher. Poor Crow! He could see the water, he could smell the water, and he could almost taste it. But he could not reach it. His bill just wasn't long enough.

Crow hopped to the ground and looked around. What could he do to get the water? Suddenly he had an idea.

A pile of small stones lay nearby on the ground. Crow picked up one stone and flew back to the table. He dropped the stone into the pitcher. Then he flew back for another stone.

One by one, Crow dropped stones into the pitcher. *Plink, plink, plunk.* With each stone, the water got a little higher. After an hour, the water was high enough for Crow to reach it. He stuck in his bill and took a long drink.

This fable teaches an important lesson: Where there's a will, there's a way. That means, if you want something enough, you can often find a way to get it.

What Are They Called?

by Ben Goode

A swarm of bees, a cloud of bats,
A gaggle of geese, a clutter of cats,

A pride of lions, a pack of dogs,
A bed of clams, a drift of hogs.

A sloth of bears, a drove of donkeys,
A school of fish, a troop of monkeys,

A herd of cows, a flock of sparrows,
A clutch of chicks,
    A murder of crows.

Retell "How Do Animals Know Where They Are Going?"

 When you retell a selection, give only the main ideas and details. Doing this helps readers understand what the selection is mostly about.

"How Do Animals Know Where They Are Going?" is an informational article. It gives facts about real life. Review the selection on pages 72–77. Look at the pictures on page 95.

■ First Picture: How do animals use landmarks? What is one animal that finds its way by landmarks?

■ The Other Four Pictures: What does the selection tell about each method? What is one animal that finds its way around by that method?

Use the pictures on page 95 to retell the selection to your partner. As you talk about each method and example, point to the correct picture. Use complete sentences.

Words you might use in your retelling:	
unique	nature
bird	fish

how animals find their way

by
landmarks

by the Sun

by
magnetism

by scent

by the stars

Dig Deeper

Look Back

Look back at the unit. It shows ways that animals meet their needs. Answer these questions on a sheet of paper.

1. What is one way that animals find their way to another place? What page shows that information?

2. What is one animal that uses a tool? What page gives that fact?

3. What problem does an animal in a fable solve? What tool does the animal use?

Talk About It

How many words can we use to describe an animal? Work with a partner. Think about an elephant.

It is big.

It is big and wrinkly.

It is big and wrinkly and has big ears.

It is big and wrinkly and has big ears and tusks.

Work together. Describe another animal. Keep adding details to your sentence.

Conversation

Sometimes you need to apologize. Maybe you have made a mistake and said something incorrectly. There is a polite way to apologize. Use the words *I'm sorry*. Tell the other person what you meant to say.

Talk to a partner. One of you will be person A. The other will be person B.

Person A

Person B

Apologize for saying something incorrectly.

Accept the apology.

Explain what you really meant to say.

Respond. Then apologize for saying something incorrectly.

Accept the apology.

Say goodbye.

Then and NOW

The **BIG** Question

How have new ways of travel changed our lives?

☐ How did people travel in the past?

☐ How did cars and airplanes change travel?

☐ Do you think people travel more now than they did long ago?

How has transportation changed from the past to today?

1. How do we talk about the past?

The past can be…

☐ a day ago.

☐ a year ago.

☐ a decade ago.

☐ a century ago.

2. How did people travel in the past?

In the past, people…

☐ rode horses.

☐ walked.

☐ sailed in boats.

☐ rode in carts.

3. How can people travel in the present?

In the present, people can travel by…

☐ car.

☐ bus.

☐ railroad train.

☐ jet.

4. What can be made on an assembly line?

On an assembly line, people can make…

☐ cars.

☐ stoves.

☐ computers.

☐ bikes.

Say **more!**

Learn the Words

travel
past
present
transportation
railroad
possible

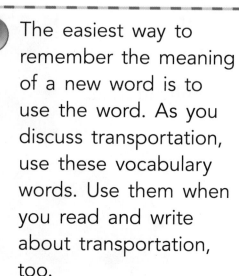

The easiest way to remember the meaning of a new word is to use the word. As you discuss transportation, use these vocabulary words. Use them when you read and write about transportation, too.

Read the word.
Look at the picture.
Listen to your teacher.

travel

past

present

transportation

railroad

possible

How Do You Feel?

Look at the vocabulary cards. Choose one picture and tell how it makes you feel.

The Haunted Basement

Marco

Angela

Nobody's home but us, Marco. Let's check out the basement.

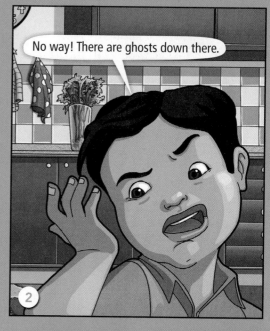

No way! There are ghosts down there.

Oh, come on. There's no such thing as ghosts.

How can you be sure?

Follow me. I'll prove it.

Angela, I hear strange sounds.

CREAK!

CREAK!

5 That's just the stairs creaking.

This place gives me the creeps. Turn the light on.

Looks like the bulb is dead.

6

But I've got to tie my shoes.

You can do it by feel. You don't have to see.

7

CLANK! CLANK!

What was that?!

8

6 **Formal/Informal Language** "This place gives me the creeps" is another way to say that the place is scary. Is this expression formal language or informal language?

105

9 Help, Angela! Something's following me!

It grabbed on to my shoe!

10

Don't freak out. It's just a can of paint.

You tied it to your shoes by accident. I'll fix it.

11

CRASH!

That's not a can of paint!

12

Of course not, Marco. It's just my old bicycle.

13

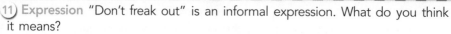

11 **Expression** "Don't freak out" is an informal expression. What do you think it means?

Look at those green eyes! That's a ghost for sure!

No, it isn't. There's nothing to be afraid of.

You're nuts! I'm leaving.

But it's not a ghost! It's just the cat!

Meow.

 17) **Formal/Informal Language** Saying that someone is "nuts," is another way to say that the person is crazy. This expression is used only in informal situations.

5,000 YEARS OF

Riverboats used oars.

Carts were built with wheels.
3500 B.C.E.

The first paved roads were built.
312 B.C.E.

Hot air balloons took to the sky.

Boats were powered by steam.
1783 C.E.

2000 B.C.E.
Horses were trained and used for **transportation**.

Ships with sails **traveled** on the ocean.

1662 C.E.
The first bus system started, with carriages pulled by horses.

TRANSPORTATION

Railroad trains were powered by steam.
1814 C.E.

People began to ride bicycles.
1863 C.E.

Helicopters!
1940 C.E.

1903 C.E.
The first airplane took flight.

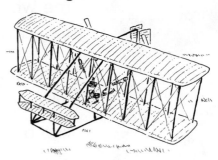

1862 C.E.
The gasoline-engine car was invented.

November 10

DEAR NEW BABY,

This is your big brother, Marco. You haven't been born yet. I am eight years old, so I know how things work around here. I've written down some rules for you.

Your room is the one on the right at the top of the stairs. Don't go left. That's my room.

Mom and Dad are the other people in the family. They're called "parents."

There's another kid besides me who hangs out here. He's not your brother. He's just my friend.

About Mom. She doesn't like it when plans change. She doesn't like being late. She hates being stuck in traffic.

Dad doesn't like loud music. Also, don't make any noise, especially when he's on the phone.

You will be born in January, which is "winter." It's cold in the winter. You won't get out very much. You will hate your snowsuit. You will want to scream when they put it on, but don't bother. Know that they will win.

I am your best friend. You can always count on me to tell you the truth and to stick up for you, no matter who you turn out to be.

Well, that's all for now. See you in two months!

Love,

Marco

The Bicycle

by Frank Long

You can be glad you didn't have to ride the first kind of bike. Back in 1865, bikes had wooden wheels and iron rims. People called them "boneshakers."

Next came a bike called a "high wheel." Its front wheel was five times higher than its back wheel. You had to be really careful on a high wheel. If you hit a rock or hole, down you went!

High wheels were dangerous. So "safety bicycles" came along. These bikes had wheels the same size. There was a problem though. Bike tires were made of solid rubber. The ride was still too bumpy.

Air-filled tires made a smooth ride possible. Bicycles became a safe and comfortable way to travel. Instead of walking, people soon rode bikes to work and school. In the early twentieth **century**, bikes were an important form of transportation.

Modern bicycles have **advanced** in many ways. They are light and fast.

In our century, bicycles are still a great way to travel. Biking is faster than walking. It is cheaper than taking the bus. Cycling saves fuel. It's kind to the planet and good for your health.

The Train

by Alex Zhang

In the **past**, most Americans didn't travel very much or very far. Railroad trains changed that.

The first railroads were built around 200 years ago. That was long before cars. Right away, railroads let people travel quickly. A trip that took two weeks by horse and wagon took only two days on a train.

The steam engine made trains **possible**. Early trains were powered by steam. Steam engines were used for about 150 years. Modern trains, however, run on electricity or diesel fuel.

In the past, trains helped our country grow. Many towns grew up beside railroad tracks. The trains carried people and goods to these new towns.

Few Americans take long train trips these days. Airplanes are faster. Cars seem more convenient. In big cities, however, millions of people still ride trains to work and school.

Modern bullet trains can travel about 300 mph! This transportation is much faster than cars. So it's possible that Americans might start taking long train trips again.

Some bullet trains can travel about 300 miles per hour.

THE CAR

by Ilona Horvath

Cars were first built in Europe in the late 1800s. After a while, Americans were making them too. Early cars were made by hand. They were very expensive.

In 1913, Henry Ford found a cheaper and faster way to make cars. He used an **assembly line** to move cars past workers. Each worker put one part on the car as it moved along.

The **purpose** of the assembly line was to save time and money. In 1908 the price of one of Ford's cars was $850. Two **decades** later, the price had fallen to $300. Low prices made it possible for many families to buy cars.

Assembly line, 1925

Cars changed the U.S. in many ways. Roads were made wider, and they were paved. Highways and bridges were built. These changes made travel easier. Also, with cars, people could live farther away from towns and cities.

Many businesses grew up around cars. Drivers needed gas stations, motels, and parking lots. Shopping centers and drive-through restaurants became popular. These businesses changed how towns and cities looked.

At **present**, the world's cheapest new car costs about $3,000. The low price lets many people own a car.

The most expensive car costs nearly $2 million. You can drive it at 250 miles per hour. But you would get a speeding ticket!

Without roads, there would be no cars.

ANOTHER Way to Go

by Duncan Searl

Grandpa hitched Daisy to the buggy in the barnyard. I climbed in. It was a beautiful Saturday to travel.

"Giddy yap," said Grandpa. The old gray horse headed out to the road.

We were going to see Aunt Ivy for her birthday. She lived in Middleville, thirty miles away. I hadn't been that far from home in five years.

"How long will the trip take?" I asked.

"We should get there in five hours," Grandpa said proudly. "If we don't have any problems."

We had a big problem, though.

It was early spring, and the road was full of mud holes. In Greenville, our buggy hit one hard. With a loud crack, one wheel broke in half.

Grandpa got out to take a look. He shook his head. "There's a blacksmith shop down the road," he said at last. "Maybe he can fix the wheel."

We led Daisy down the road to the shop. "Sure, I can fix it," said the blacksmith. "But not until Monday."

"But we have to get to Middleville," I said. "It's Aunt Ivy's birthday."

"Hmm. Middleville," said the blacksmith. "Well, I just saw Dr. Owens. He's heading over there this morning. Maybe you can ride with him."

Dr. Owens listened to our story. "Of course you can ride with me," he said. "I was just about to leave."

"Where's your horse?" Grandpa asked.

"Don't need one," the doctor said with a smile. He led us to the back of his house.

There it was—a bright red horseless carriage. I had never even seen one. It was still the first decade of the new century.

Grandpa frowned at the modern machine. He had never seen one either. "Are you sure it will make it all the way to Middleville?"

Zoom In

What details from the story and the pictures help you infer what a "horseless carriage" really is?

The doctor smiled again. He was turning a crank to start the engine. Suddenly the machine gave a loud roar. Grandpa and I jumped. "Get in," said the doctor. "We'll see."

Out on the road, clouds of dust swirled around us. "This is a very advanced engine," the doctor said proudly. "It can go twelve miles an hour."

Grandpa shook his head. "That doesn't seem possible!"

We passed a horse and wagon. I looked back at the driver. Suddenly I felt as if he was living in the past. I was riding into the future.

I looked at Grandpa. I didn't think he would like the ride. He was smiling, though, and asking questions. "Is it hard to learn to drive?" he asked. "What's the purpose of this knob? Who fixes it if it breaks?"

We reached Middleville in less than three hours. The doctor drove us right to Aunt Ivy's house. It was hard to believe.

Aunt Ivy was sitting on the porch. Her eyes popped when she saw us. My cousin Jimmy ran out to touch the engine. The baby started crying.

After the birthday party, Grandpa and Aunt Ivy sat down to talk. "We'll have to stay till Monday," Grandpa said. "That's when the buggy will be ready."

"To get back home, you can take the railroad to High Falls," Aunt Ivy said. "Then you'll have to walk three miles over the hill to reach Green Village. There's no other way to go."

"Oh, there's another way to go," said Grandpa, smiling. "I could get a horseless carriage!"

Prove It

Does Grandpa like the horseless carriage? How do you know from the story?

Plenty of Ways to Go

by Duncan Searl

"What!" I shouted at my mother. "You've got to be kidding! How can we live in the twenty-first century without a car?"

Our old car had broken down. "It's not worth fixing," Mom said. "Besides, I don't have the money. Don't worry. It's possible to live without a car."

I wasn't so sure. "How are we going to get to my piano lesson tomorrow?" I suddenly asked.

"There are plenty of ways to go, Lena," Mom said. "There's public transportation, for example. Or maybe we could ride our bikes."

The next morning I dusted off my bike. I hadn't ridden it in months. I always thought bikes were just for fun. Now I saw they had a purpose.

Bikes are slower than cars. That's not always bad. On a bike, you see and hear more than in a car. Mom and I passed a big park and a city swimming pool. We waved to other bike riders. Riding bikes was a fun way to travel.

On the way home from my piano lesson, we rode through a park.

On Sundays we go shopping. In the past, we always drove out to a big shopping center off the highway. This Sunday we took the bus downtown.

"I've never been on a city bus," I said.

"There's no time like the present," Mom said.

The bus was a modern one. It was cool and clean inside. Mom was sitting next to a woman with a violin. They started to talk. The woman was playing at a free concert in the park. She invited us to come.

"Let's go to the concert," Mom said to me. "We can go shopping anytime."

So by taking the bus, we got to hear some great music.

Thanksgiving rolled around. We wanted to go to Grandma's house in Portland.

"How are we going to get to Oregon?" I asked. We still didn't have a car.

"There's a thing called a railroad," she laughed.

The train trip was really fun. It was a high-speed train. So we went over 90 mph. We watched a movie together on Mom's laptop. Then we ordered lunch and took a nap. I think I could get used to traveling by train.

Mom and I haven't had a car for over six months now. Believe it or not, it hasn't been so bad.

We know all the bus routes in town and plan our trips around them. We often ride our bikes or walk. As a result, we're both in better shape.

Not having a car has saved us money, too. We've decided to use the money to try another type of transportation. In April, we're flying across the country to Washington, DC.

So what Mom said last summer is really true: There's more than one way to go!

Prove It

How did Lena's feelings about cars change through the story? What details helped you answer?

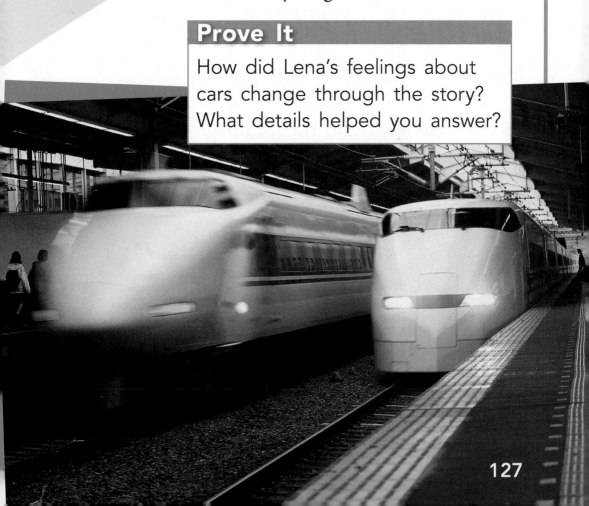

The Transportation Century

by Sonia Lee

Transportation changed *quickly* during the twentieth century. Back in 1900, most people still used horses to travel. Horses pulled people in carriages. Horse-drawn wagons delivered goods to homes and businesses. In the past, city buses were even pulled by horses.

In the decades after 1900, most cities got electric streetcars. These streetcars were also called trolleys. Trolleys traveled over rails in the streets. Electric lines overhead powered the trolleys.

New York City opened the first American subway in 1904. Subway trains travel through tunnels underground.

In 1900, the United States had dozens of railroads. In all, there were 200,000 miles of train tracks. All cities and most large towns had a railroad station.

Trains weren't that fast in 1900. Most went between 25 and 40 miles an hour. Still, it was the best way to travel long distances.

Cars were still new at the turn of the century. There were only 8,000 cars in the United States in 1900. Few roads were paved. So dust and mud made driving difficult.

Out in the country, people still used horses. There weren't any other ways to get around.

The first decades of the century brought other changes to transportation. The most important change was the rise of the automobile.

Thanks to assembly lines, cars became cheaper after 1910. More and more Americans could buy them. By 1920, one in five Americans owned a car. By 1950, nearly 100 million cars were on our roads.

How did cars change travel? For one thing, horses were rarely seen on the streets anymore. Bicycles were less common, too. People also took fewer long trips by train. When it came to traveling, people wanted to drive their cars.

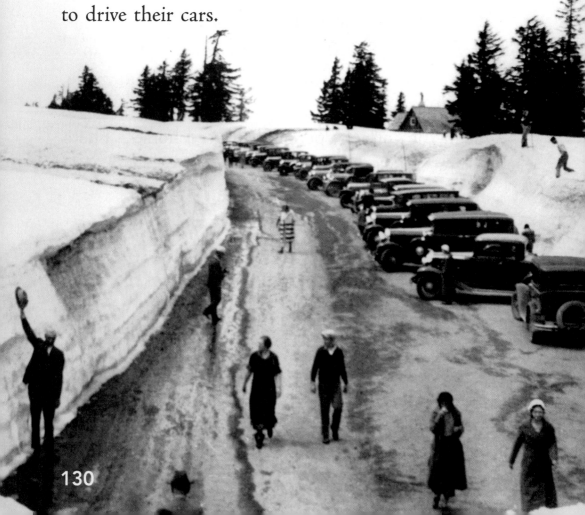

The Wright brothers invented the airplane in 1903. Within several decades, air travel became widespread.

In 1919, an airplane flew from England to France. It was the first plane to carry passengers. In 1933, a 12-passenger airplane came off the assembly line.

The first jet airplanes flew in 1937. Jets made air travel much faster. The airline business grew.

By 1950, the sky was full of travelers. For the first time, more Americans traveled by plane than by train.

Zoom In

What detail can help you infer that the size of airplanes got larger several decades after the first airplane?

The second half of the century saw more advanced transportation. For the first time, people traveled into space.

In 1969, an American spacecraft rocketed to the moon. *Apollo 11* carried three men aboard. Two of them walked on the moon. Over the next few years, six more moon landings took place.

The space shuttle is a cross between a rocket and an airplane. It is another way to travel into space. Between 1981 and 2011, travelers on space shuttles made more than 100 trips.

Spacecraft without people have traveled to Mars and other planets. Will it be possible for us to go to these places someday?

Transportation changed so much during the last century. It's likely to keep on changing in this one.

Some cars, for example, can now

drive themselves. Will they become more common as time goes by? Perhaps cars may be able to fly someday.

Maybe people will start wearing jetpacks. Then we all could fly.

No one knows for sure how transportation will change. But we can be sure that traveling faster and farther is something most people want to do.

Prove It

What types of new transportation does the author think may be invented in this century? What is your evidence?

modern

assembly line

advanced

century

decade

purpose

- Read the words on the list.
- Read the dialogue.
- Find the words.

A new auto parts plant will be built here.

Good! This building has been empty for a **decade**.

1. Draw Your Dream Car
Listening and Speaking

Work with a partner. Think about the auto parts plant from the picture above. What kind of new car would you like this plant to work on? Make a drawing. Tell your partner about your car. Tell what is special about it.

2. Make a Venn Diagram
Graphic Organizer

Work with a partner. Think about ways in which cars and buses are alike and different. In the left oval, write facts that are true about cars only. In the right oval, write facts that are true about buses only. In the center, write facts that are true about both.

Compare Cars and Buses

cars   both   buses

3. Write About the Future
Writing

Think about the next decade. What kinds of transportation will be invented or made better? Think about trains, cars, planes, and space travel. Write a paragraph. Show your paragraph to your partner.

4. You Are the Actor
Listening and Speaking

Work with a partner. Take turns reading the dialogue in the picture above. Ask your partner about any words you don't understand. Then use your best acting voice. Make the dialogue come alive.

Travel Tips

by Emma Blanco

Before you go to somewhere else,

You have to understand,

There are no trains
that cross the sea,

And ships don't
work on land.

A plane won't get
you to the store,

A bike won't fly to Spain.

There are no cars
that climb up trees

Or climb back down again.

The Moondust Footprint

(Joshua Katz,
Woodstock, Vermont,
July 20, 1969)

by Bobbi Katz

We'd been watching, watching, watching
all day long into the night:
    Mission Control in Houston,
        Apollo astronauts in flight.
A new chapter of history
    was about to open soon.
The Apollo slowed . . . then quickened,
speeding closer to the moon.

The others went to bed,
but not Aunt Mary and me.
We kept watching, watching, watching
    each slow stage on the TV:
        the hovering Landing Module,
            the Sea of Tranquillity,
                and the astronaut, Neil Armstrong,
                    moving oh so carefully . . .

I was holding my breath
    —Aunt Mary said she'd held hers, too—
until we saw the moondust footprint
    made by Armstrong's ribbed left shoe!

That footprint marked a moment—
    an awesome human victory.
We were watching history happen,
    my aunt Mary . . . and me.

Retell "Another Way to Go"

> When you retell a story, you tell only the main important parts or events. Sometimes you can tell about a problem the characters have. You can tell how they try to solve it. You can tell how things end up.

"Another Way to Go" is a story. The characters have a problem. They come up with a solution. Review the selection on pages 118–123. The chart on page 141 shows what happens.

■ **Top Row:** What problem do the characters have?

■ **Middle Row:** What do the characters decide to do?

■ **Bottom Row:** What happens at the end of the story?

Use the pictures on page 141 to retell the story to your partner. As you tell about each part, point to the correct picture. Use complete sentences.

Words you might use in your retelling:	
travel	transportation
possible	purpose

problem

solution

outcome

Dig Deeper

Look Back

Look at "Another Way to Go" and "Plenty of Ways to Go." Both stories are written by the same author. Answer these questions on a sheet of paper.

1. Who is the main character in each story?

2. What do both main characters learn that is the same in both stories?

3. How is the setting of each story different?

Talk About It

What was transportation like in the past?

At first, people traveled by foot, on horseback, or in boats.

Then the train was invented.

Next came the car and then the airplane.

Finally, people could travel into outer space.

In your own words, tell about how something else has changed. Use *first, next,* and *finally.*

Conversation

> **ⓘ** Some words help you show respect for others. Say *please* when you ask for something. Say *thank you* when someone helps you. Say *excuse me* when you need to interrupt someone.

Talk to a partner. One of you will be person A. The other will be person B.

Person A   **Person B**

Ask for something politely.

Respond.

Thank your partner.
Ask a question.

Interrupt your partner's question politely.
Ask for something.

Respond.

Thank your partner.

Making Life Easier

The BIG Question

How has technology changed our world?

☐ How did people stay in touch many years ago?

☐ How do most people communicate now?

☐ How do you think people will communicate in the future?

What tools and machines do we use?

1. What are some parts of a computer?

A computer has…

☐ a monitor.

☐ a mouse.

☐ a keyboard.

☐ a printer.

2. What things do people use every day?

People use…

☐ wheels.

☐ calculators.

☐ metal tools.

☐ electricity.

3. What machines or tools use electricity?

You need electricity for...

☐ a computer.

☐ a lamp.

☐ a TV set.

☐ a refrigerator.

4. How can you share your thoughts with others?

You can...

☐ type on a laptop.

☐ write with a pen.

☐ speak.

☐ sing.

Say **more!**

Learn the Words

calculator

monitor

keyboard

computer

printer

type

Theme Vocabulary

> **ⓘ** The easiest way to remember the meaning of a new word is to use the word. As you discuss technology, use these vocabulary words. Use them when you read and write about technology, too.
>
> **Read** the word.
> **Look** at the picture.
> **Listen** to your teacher.

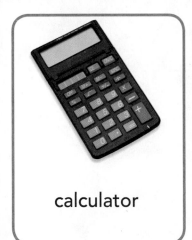

calculator

monitor

keyboard

computer

printer

type

Match the Pictures

Look at the pictures on the vocabulary cards. Choose two pictures that go together. Tell why you think the pictures go together.

Zhen **Mei** **Pablo** **Mom**

2 **Expressions** When the girl says, "I'm afraid you can't come home with me," she means that she is sorry she can't bring the dog home.

151

 13) **Formal/Informal Language** When the man calls the girl "young lady," is he using formal or informal language?

152

 19 **Formal/Informal Language** "My apologies once again" is formal language. How could he say this in an informal way?

Where's Bossy?

by Duncan Searl

"Bossy?" Zhen called. "Bossy!" She couldn't find her new puppy. Bossy wasn't in the kitchen or the living room. So Zhen raced upstairs.

Mom was at her **computer monitor**. She was working on a **report**. "I can't find Bossy," Zhen said.

"Look outside in the yard," Mom said. Zhen hurried back downstairs and opened the front door. The front gate was open. Had Bossy gotten out?

Zhen looked up and down the street. She ran to the corner. There was no sign of Bossy.

Zhen rushed home. "Mom!" she shouted. "Bossy got loose. The front gate was open."

Mom kept **typing commands** on her **keyboard**. Her **printer** began to hum. "Mom, PLEASE!" Zhen cried.

"Did you look outside?" asked Mom.

"I told you," Zhen said. "He's not in the front yard."

"What about the backyard?" Mom asked.

"Bossy doesn't like the backyard," Zhen said.

"He does now," said Mom.

Mom and Zhen went out back. There was Bossy—sleeping in his brand-new house.

"I got the house today when you were at school," Mom explained. "Bossy likes it so much, he won't come out!"

Prove It

How did Mom help Zhen? Tell how you know.

Getting Things Done

by Li Yan Tan

Materials Needed:
marker pens, poster paper

Do you ever get the feeling you have too much to do? If so, you're not alone.

Making a list is a good idea. But lists don't always work. Some things need to be done right away, while others can wait. A list doesn't tell you what to do <u>first</u>.

A circle graph can help you organize your tasks. It helps you make decisions about what has to be done right away and what can wait.

Directions:

1. Make a big circle on a sheet of paper.
2. Divide it into three sections.
3. Label them as I show on my circle graph.
4. Number them, too.

Here's How It Works:

- Things that are "Important and Urgent" will get your attention now.

- Things that are "Important and Not Urgent" can be done later.

- Things that are "Not Important and Not Urgent" can be done whenever you get to them.

Now, it's your turn!

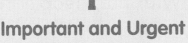

1
Important and Urgent
find eyeglasses
bring in permission slip
return library books
do homework

2
**Important and
Not Urgent**
clean backpack
write thank-you note
practice guitar

3
**Not Important
and Not Urgent**
call Keira
arrange CDs

Fire

by Talia Rodriguez

It was many thousands of years ago. Lightning struck a dead tree. A family gathered around the burning tree for warmth. One of the people picked up a burning branch and carried it to another dead tree. The secret was out!

The discovery of fire was a great event. Fire was a very useful tool—for warmth, cooking, and safety. With fire, people lived better and longer lives.

Fire was so important that people had to explain it. They told stories about how people first got fire. Native Americans on the Pacific Coast told this myth.

Raven Brings Fire

Long ago, people lived in darkness. They were cold and afraid. At that time, Gray Eagle owned the Sun, the Moon, and fire. He kept them in his house in the sky and would not share them.

Raven was a young man. He felt sorry for the people. So he changed himself into a white bird and flew up to talk to Gray Eagle.

Inside Gray Eagle's house, Raven saw the Sun, the Moon, and fire. "I must bring these things down to the people!" Raven decided.

So Raven stole the Sun and Moon. He stole a burning log, too. Then Raven flew back to Earth.

Along the way, Raven hung the Sun in the sky. Now people could plant crops. Raven also hung the Moon. Now people could see at night.

The burning log burned Raven. So, Raven dropped the log onto some rocks. The fire went into the rocks. Now people could make fire by striking these rocks together.

Six Simple Machines

by Michael Ellis

Computers, **calculators**, and **robots** are modern machines. They have many parts and use **electricity**.

But any device that can do work is a machine. These six simple machines are thousands of years old. They do many **chores** that make our lives easier.

Wheel and Axle

An axle is a rod through the center of a wheel. A wheel and axle make it easier to move loads.

Lever and Fulcrum

A lever is a stiff bar. A lever rests on a fixed point called a fulcrum. A lever is used to lift things or pry them loose. In one type of lever you push down on the bar. The lever does the work of lifting.

Inclined Plane

An inclined plane is a flat surface raised at one end. An inclined plane makes it easier to move things from a lower place to a higher place, or from a higher place to a lower place.

Screw

A screw is an inclined plane wrapped around a cylinder or cone. Screws are often used to hold things together.

Pulley

A pulley is a wheel that has a rope wrapped around it. Pulleys are used to raise, lower, or lift something.

Wedge

A wedge is wide at one end and narrow at the other. A wedge is used to cut or split something apart.

Finding Simple Machines

by Anna Torres

People use the six simple machines every day. You can find these machines at work in all kinds of places. You'll even see them in your local park.

At the playground, some children **plan** to play on a slide. One end of the slide is six feet high. The other end is near the ground. The children reach the bottom quickly. What type of simple machine helps them?

Two children are on a seesaw. On it, each one can easily lift the weight of the other. What type of machine is a seesaw?

Some children are riding their skateboards. What simple machine helps the skateboards move so quickly?

A park worker is raising the flag on a flagpole. When she pulls on the rope, the flag slides easily up the pole. That's because the rope goes around a simple machine near the top of the flagpole. What is it?

A runner stops for a drink of water. After drinking, he turns the lid back on his water bottle until it is tight. What simple machine holds the lid on the water bottle?

At the picnic table, a woman is eating. She uses the cutting edge of a knife to cut up her food. What simple machine is she using?

Robert

by Deborah March

A few weeks ago, Dad had a great idea. He thought that we should get a robot. I thought it was a great idea, too. How cool would that be? The robot could play all kinds of games with me. It could even play ball with me when Dad was busy. It could clean up my room. I would never have to make my bed again. Best of all, it could do my homework! Robots probably always get the answers to math problems right.

the Robot

Dad had a different plan. He thought the robot could go food shopping and drive me to school. It could cook our dinner—while I did my homework.

I tried to argue with Dad. "I'll get much better grades if a robot helps me with my homework," I pointed out.

"You get good grades when you work hard," Dad said. "Homework helps you get smarter. A robot is already smart. It doesn't need homework."

I saw that Dad wasn't going to change his mind.

Zoom In

Who are the characters in this story so far?

165

We drove to the mall and then walked to the store with the sensible robots. We went right past the fun stores. Dad said no to dancing robots, flying robots, and joking robots. He said yes to Robert the Robot.

From the minute I met Robert, he was boring. All he thought about was work, health, and safety.

"Shall I drive you home, sir?" he asked Dad. "I can drive any make of car. Be sure you close the car door tightly after sitting down."

He made a beeping sound and added, "My weather app shows that the temperature is low today. Perhaps you both should button up your coats."

By the time the car drove into our garage, I had had it with Robert. "Lighten up, Robert," I said.

He just looked at me and pointed to the tiny screen on his shoulder. It said 175 pounds. "This is my weight," he said. "I cannot make myself any lighter. I also know that humans cannot make themselves lighter in just a few minutes. In fact, there is no living thing that can make itself lighter that quickly."

"Never mind!" I said grumpily.

When we walked into the house, Dad went to his office with Robert. I knew that he was giving the robot chores to do. I went to my room and turned on my 3-D computer. But Robert came back almost right away.

"I have a great deal of work to do," the robot said. "While I'm busy cleaning and cooking, you should do your homework."

I could have screamed.

Zoom In

What clues tell you that this story could not take place in real life in the present?

Our new robot got to work. He zoomed around the kitchen, cleaning the stove and washing the pans left from lunch. Good. Those were chores I wouldn't have to do. Then he zipped around the living room with the vacuum cleaner. By the time he finished, there was not a speck of dust to be found.

But I still had to make my own bed.

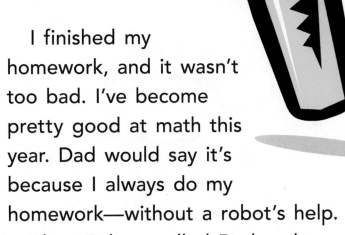

I finished my homework, and it wasn't too bad. I've become pretty good at math this year. Dad would say it's because I always do my homework—without a robot's help.

Then Robert called Dad and me for dinner. We were in for a shock. Robert was a great cook! It was the best dinner I ever had.

Dad thought so too. He smiled at me and said, "A flying robot couldn't make noodle soup this good, could he?"

I had to say he was right.

The next morning, after Robert made us a delicious breakfast, he drove me to school. He didn't drive very fast, but he took a different road from the one Dad usually took. We reached the school in time for me to hang out with my friends before class.

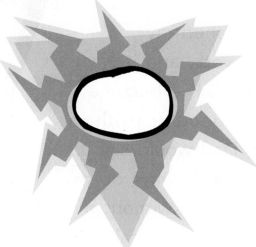

Robert was waiting in the car after school. "You have forgotten your backpack," he said.

He was right! I ran back inside and found it in my classroom. I picked it up and went back out to our car. Robert was waiting for me.

"You know, Robert," I said on the way home, "you're not so bad after all."

Prove It

How do the writer's feelings about Robert change during the story?

Words on Paper

by Peggy Marsden

People have been writing things down for a long time. At first, they wrote on clay tablets with a pointed stick. This was about 5,000 years ago, in what is now Iraq.

About the same time, people in Egypt invented papyrus. To make it, they cut up plants called reeds. Then they soaked the reeds and pounded them flat. The result was a thin sheet of writing material. In other places, people wrote on dried animal skins.

About 2,000 years ago, the Chinese invented paper. To make it, they mixed plant fibers and rags.

The Chinese also invented printing blocks. First, they carved the words for a page onto a block of wood. Next, they coated the block with ink. Then they pressed the block onto a piece of paper. With this block, they could print the same page over and over.

Later inventors placed each letter of the alphabet on a small piece of metal. These pieces of metal were called type. The type could be moved around to form words. The machine that held this type was called a printing press. Now people could print the same book again and again. They didn't have to write each one by hand.

an early printing press ▲

Type changed the way books were made. At home and work, however, people still had to write by hand. For over a thousand years, people used quill pens. Quill pens were the feathers of large birds. To write, you dipped the tip of the quill in ink.

Dipping a pen in ink over and over was slow, messy work. In 1883, a new invention changed that. The fountain pen had its own ink supply inside. Fountain pens made writing easier.

Today most people use ballpoint pens. They became popular in the 1940s. People like ballpoints because they are cheap and easy to use.

Zoom In

In what ways did the pen change over time?

The typewriter was invented in 1873. With a typewriter, words were neat and easy to read. Using a typewriter was also faster than writing by hand. Writing became less of a chore.

Typewriters changed people's lives. In offices, workers could get more work done in less time. At home, people wrote more—letters, stories, everything!

Typewriters were used all around the world for about a hundred years. Then a machine that was even faster and more useful took over. The world turned to the computer.

Computers have been in use since the 1940s. Early ones were huge, expensive, and hard to use.

Personal computers became popular in the 1980s. They were small and easy to use. Personal computers had keyboards, and many people used them to write. They viewed their words on the screen of a monitor.

A computer lets you correct your work as you write. If you're fixing a long report, you don't have to start all over again. There are **commands** on the keyboard for all sorts of helpful tasks.

When you've finished writing, you can print what you have written onto paper. With a printer, you can make dozens of copies. And you always have a record of what you wrote.

Great Inventions in Communications

Tape Recorder—1935

Photocopier—1938

Videotape—1956

Computer Chip—1959

Word Processor—1964

Fax Machine—1964

Personal Computer—1978

Compact Disk (CD)—1981

How are you?

Today, cell phones and tablets are helping people get their words down.

Early mobile phones were first used in the 1950s and 1960s. These phones were used mainly in cars. By the 1990s, handheld cell phones were in wide use. The first text message was sent in 1992.

A tablet is a computer you can take with you anywhere. It's smaller than a laptop but bigger than a cell phone. People use tablets to text and to write e-mails, letters, and reports.

From clay tablets to computer tablets—writing has come a long way!

Great!
How about you?

Prove It

How do personal computers make writing easier than it is with a typewriter or a pen? What evidence did you use?

robot

chore

command

plan

report

electricity

- Read the words on the list.
- Read the dialogue.
- Find the words.

I like the **robot**. It looks like a real one. Julio and Lee are doing a good job.

1. What Are They Doing?
Writing

The children in the picture above are all making things. Get ready to interview one or more of the children. Ask them about what they are making. Write five questions to ask the child or children. Exchange questions with your partner. Ask about any words you don't understand in your partner's questions.

2. What Kind of Robot?
Graphic Organizer

Ask a few friends. What kind of robot would they want? What task would their robot do? Take a survey. Tally the answers. Share your findings with your partner.

What Kind of Robot
Do You Want?

A Robot That...	Votes
does chores	
plays computer games	
explains schoolwork	
drives a car	

We have one more hour to work on our crafts. Then I must clean up the room. Maybe you will help me with that **chore**.

Do you think robots work on **electricity**?

Julio and Lee followed the **plan** from the robot kit.

I will write the **report** about it.

Someday I'll make a real robot. It will follow every **command** I give it.

3. You Are the Actor
Listening and Speaking

Work with a partner. Take turns reading the dialogue in the picture above. First, ask your partner about any words you don't understand. When you read, use your best acting voice. Make the dialogue come alive.

4. Make a List
Vocabulary

Work with a partner. Name as many things as you can that run on electricity. Share your list with the class. See which pair has the longest list.

What Runs on Electricity?

Keeping in Touch

by William Huggins

A horse and rider dashed along a trail. The rider carried a bag of mail. He changed horses every ten miles. After riding a hundred miles, he handed the mail to another rider. In 1860, this was a new way to get mail—the Pony Express.

The Pony Express route began in St. Joseph, Missouri, near the Missouri River. Riders raced westward to Sacramento, California. From there, the mail traveled downriver to San Francisco.

In all, the Pony Express route was about 1,900 miles. The riders covered the distance in ten days. That was a speed record in 1860.

The Pony Express lasted for only a year and a half. That's because a new invention replaced it.

The telegraph used electricity to send messages across wires. However, in order for people to send telegrams, wires had to be put up. It took years to put up poles and wires all across the country. That's why the Pony Express was so important in 1860. It was the only fast overland communication to the West Coast at the time. Then, in 1861, California was connected to the rest of the country by telegraph.

Telegraph messages traveled fast over the wires. Someone had to send and receive them, though. Then they had to be delivered. So getting a telegraph could take a day or two. It was still faster than anything else, even the Pony Express.

The telephone was an improvement over the telegraph because people could hear each other's voices. Starting in the 1840s, many people worked on its invention. Like the telegraph, the telephone needed electrical wires to carry its signals. So people couldn't have telephones until wires were put up in their communities.

The first coast-to-coast long distance telephone call was made in 1915. In time, phone calls replaced telegrams.

In time, better phones were invented. At first, phones connected to the wall by a fixed wire. Then came the cordless phone. People could carry this phone from room to room in their home.

The mobile phone, or cell phone, could really move. Now people can carry their phones all across the country. They just have to remember to recharge the battery!

These days, it doesn't take ten days to get a message to your friends. You can keep in touch with anyone, anywhere, in seconds. Technology has made it easier for people to communicate.

Today people make fewer phone calls. They tend to text, e-mail, or Skype instead. Will new inventions replace e-mail and texting some day? It's hard to imagine what they might be. Still, people are always looking for better ways to say what's on their mind.

Prove It

What are some ways the telephone was improved over time? Which text and photographs helped you answer?

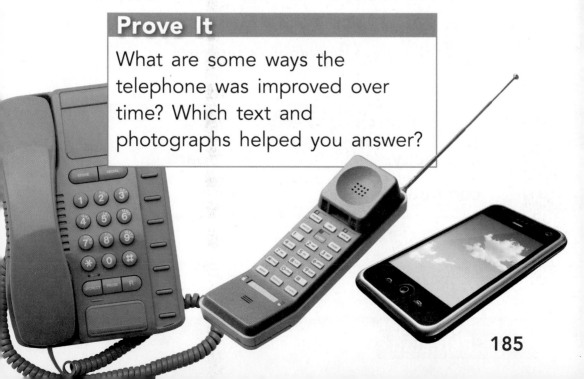

Retell "Words on Paper"

 When you retell a selection about events that take place in time order, you tell about the events in order.

"Words on Paper" tells about what people have used to write things down over many years. Review the selection on pages 174–179. Look at the pictures on page 187.

■ First Picture: What did people use to write with first?

■ Second Picture: What was invented later?

■ Third Picture: What is the latest invention?

Use the pictures on page 187 to retell the story to your partner. As you tell about each invention, point to the correct picture. Use complete sentences.

Words you might use in your retelling:	
electricity	keyboard
computer	chore

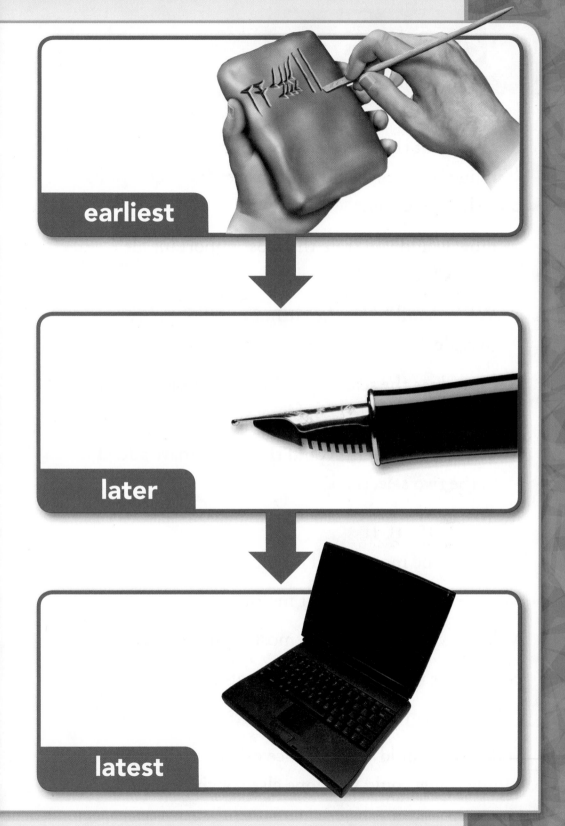

earliest

later

latest

Dig Deeper

Look Back

Look back at the selections "Six Simple Machines" and "Finding Simple Machines." Answer these questions on a sheet of paper.

1. How would you state the most important idea of "Six Simple Machines"?

2. What details does the author use to support that idea?

3. How does the selection "Finding Simple Machines" help readers understand how simple machines work?

4. What other details could the author have added to the two selections?

Talk About It

Which is the most useful invention of all time?

Write a description of that invention.

Why do you think it is the most useful invention?

Share your idea with your classmates.

Do you all agree? Why or why not?

If not, how could you convince others to change their minds? How could someone else convince you?

Conversation

> Sometimes a friend asks you how to do something. Then you need to give clear **instructions.** Always give each step in order. Use words like *first, second, next,* and *finally.*

Talk to a partner. One of you will be person A. The other will be person B.

Person A

Tell the first step of how to do something.

Tell the next step.

Give the correct third step if your partner was wrong.

Person B

Ask what you need to do next.

Guess the third step. Tell your partner.

Thank your partner.

Shoot for the Stars

The BIG Question

Why is it important to learn about the universe? How do we explore it?

☐ When you look up at the night sky, what do you see?

☐ Why do astronauts travel into outer space?

☐ What do you think astronauts might learn?

Let's Talk

What do we know about outer space?

1. What can you see in outer space?

In outer space, I can see...

- ☐ other planets.
- ☐ the Moon.
- ☐ the Sun.
- ☐ many, many stars.

2. What do astronauts do?

Astronauts...

- ☐ train hard for their job.
- ☐ wear big suits with helmets.
- ☐ fly into space.
- ☐ spend time in the space shuttle.

3. What is it like in outer space?

In outer space...

☐ there is no air.

☐ there are many stars.

☐ there are big and small planets.

4. What other planets orbit the Sun?

Planets in our solar system include...

☐ Venus.

☐ Mars.

☐ Jupiter.

☐ Saturn.

Say more!

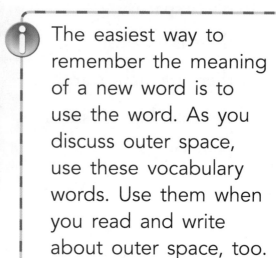

Learn the Words

solar system
planet
orbit
phase
outer space
astronaut

Theme Vocabulary

i The easiest way to remember the meaning of a new word is to use the word. As you discuss outer space, use these vocabulary words. Use them when you read and write about outer space, too.

Read the word.
Look at the picture.
Listen to your teacher.

solar system

planet

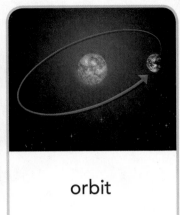

orbit

phase

outer space

astronaut

Match the Pictures

Look at the pictures on the vocabulary cards. Choose two pictures that go together. Tell why you think the pictures go together.

COOKING DINNER

 Feng   **Min**  **Mom**

1 Mom's still at work, so I'm going to cook dinner.

Do you know how?

Nothing to it.

2 I just grab what's on the shelf and cook it. Piece of cake.

3 Mom said not to mess with the stove.

Okay. We'll just put something together. Mom can cook it when she gets home.

4 We could make some noodles.

5 That's the spirit!

More like a cup.

Does ketchup work?

Yes! We'll have noodles with red sauce!

Make sure to use all of it.

Perfect! I'll just stir it up and leave it on the counter.

Now we can kick back and wait for Mom.

 14 **Formal/Informal Language** "Now we can kick back" is an informal expression. What do you think it means?

198

17 **Formal/Informal Language** "This noodle soup rocks!" is informal language. How could you say the same thing in a more formal way?

199

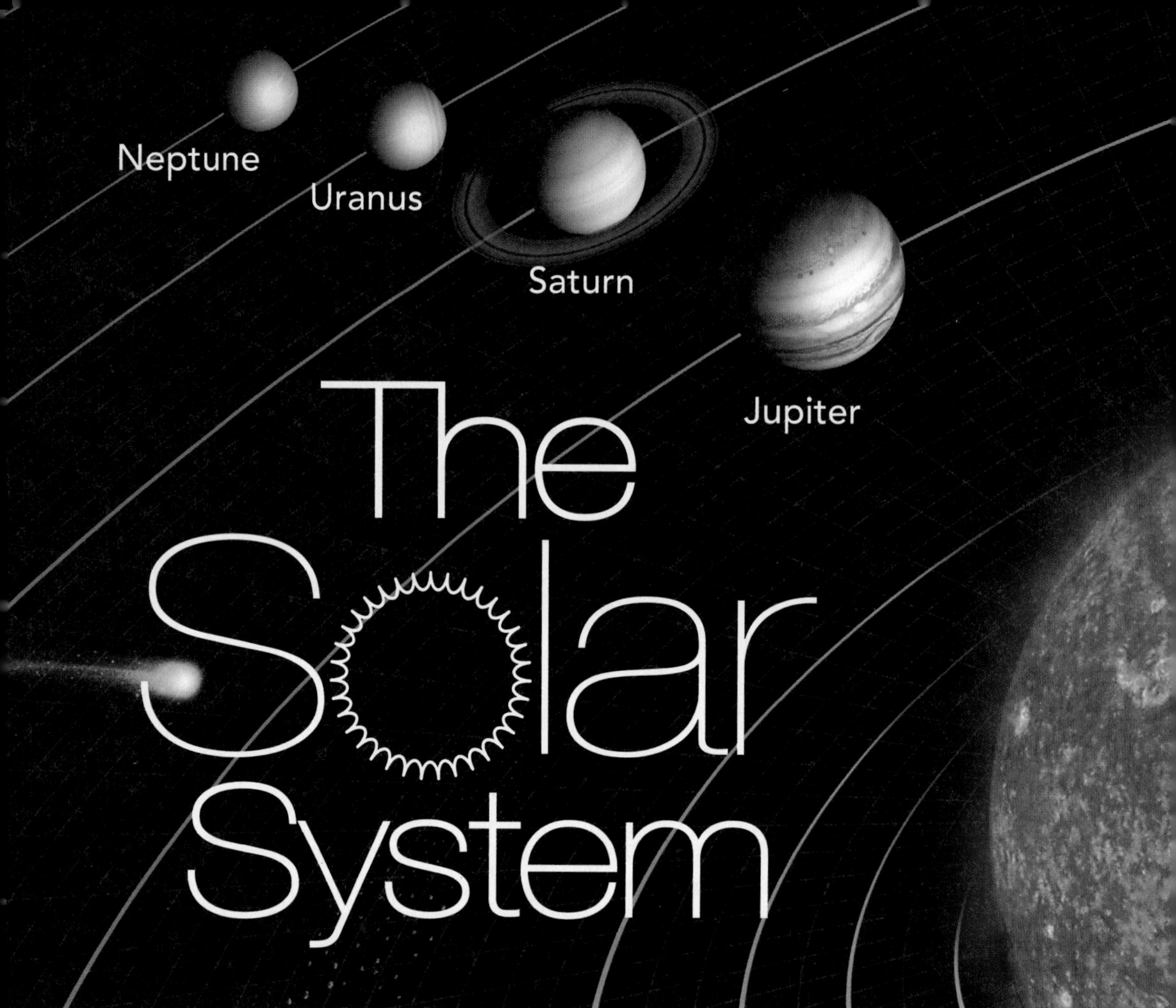

Neptune

Uranus

Saturn

Jupiter

The Solar System

All the **planets** in the **solar system** travel in paths that circle the Sun. The Sun is the center.

People say the Sun rises in the morning and sets at night. That makes it sound as if the Sun is moving. It is really Earth and the other planets that move.

Earth takes one year to orbit the Sun. Planets that are closer to the Sun take less time to circle the Sun.

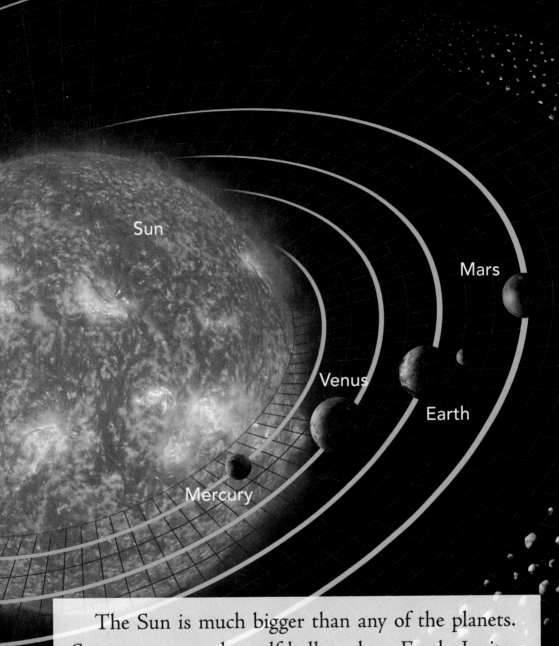

Sun

Mars

Venus

Earth

Mercury

The Sun is much bigger than any of the planets. Suppose you used a golf ball to show Earth. Jupiter would be the size of a beach ball. The Sun would be a ball nearly 14 feet across. If the Sun were hollow, about one million Earths could fit inside it!

Report

What's Up with Pluto?

by Nela Melendez

Planets are spheres that orbit the Sun. They are large enough to make a path around the Sun without other objects pulling them out of their orbit.

In 1906, scientists believed there were eight planets. In 1930, scientists in Arizona spotted a new object that they named Planet X. Two months later, Planet X was renamed Pluto, after a Roman god.

Sun   Mercury   Venus   Earth   Mars

For years, people thought that there were nine planets. They came up with a saying that helped them remember the order of the nine planets from the Sun.

My	Very	Excellent		Mother	Just	Sent	Us	Nine	Pizzas.
Ⓜ	Ⓥ	Ⓔ		Ⓜ	Ⓙ	Ⓢ	Ⓤ	Ⓝ	Ⓟ
e	e	a		a	u	a	r	e	l
r	n	r		r	p	t	a	p	u
c	u	t		s	i	u	n	t	t
u	s	h			t	r	u	u	o
r					e	n	s	n	
y					r			e	

However, on August 24, 2006, scientists decided that Pluto wasn't really a planet after all. It is now called a dwarf planet. So how should that handy saying be revised?

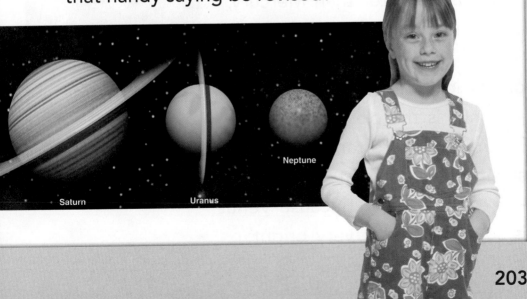

Neptune

Saturn   Uranus

The Planets

Mercury

by Paul Toussaint

Mercury is the closest planet to the Sun. During the day, Mercury is hotter than an oven. The temperature can reach 800°F. At night, the temperature can fall to 280°F below zero. That's colder than anywhere on Earth.

Like all planets, Mercury spins to go from day to night. Mercury spins slowly, though. It takes 69 Earth days for Mercury to go from day to night.

Venus

Venus is hotter than Mercury, even though it's farther from the Sun. In fact, it's the hottest planet in the solar system.

Venus is the closest planet to Earth. You can often see Venus shining in the sky at dawn or in the early evening. Because Venus is so close by, it's very bright.

Earth

This is where you live! It's also the only planet where you could live. Do you know why?

For one thing, Earth is the only planet with liquid water on its surface. Also, no other planet has as much oxygen for breathing.

Without water and oxygen, life as we know it could not exist.

Mars

Like Earth, Mars has ice caps at its north and south poles. Mars is much colder than Earth, though.

Mars is farther from the Sun than Earth. So its orbit around the Sun takes longer. A year on Mars is almost two Earth years.

Zoom In

What two details explain why life can exist on Earth?

Jupiter

Jupiter is the largest planet. Its surface is made of gas. Storms swirl around it at hundreds of miles per hour. Jupiter has 63 moons, more than any other planet.

Jupiter has a long orbit around the Sun. A year on Jupiter is 4,331 Earth days. Jupiter spins faster than Earth, though. So a day on Jupiter is less than 10 hours.

Saturn

Many people think Saturn is the most beautiful planet. That's because Saturn is surrounded by three bright rings and many smaller ones.

The rings of Saturn are formed from ice, rocks, and dust. The planet itself is a ball of gas. If you had a tub of water large enough, Saturn would float in it!

Uranus

Uranus is the seventh planet from the Sun. It's so far away that you need a telescope to see it. Uranus is the coldest planet and has very strong winds.

Like Saturn, Uranus is a ball of gas. The gas at its core is frozen solid. Uranus also has rings, but they are much thinner than Saturn's.

Neptune

Neptune is the farthest planet from the Sun. As a result, it takes Neptune 165 Earth years to orbit the Sun.

Neptune has the strongest winds in the solar system. Some of its winds move at more than 1,000 miles per hour.

Twelve of Neptune's thirteen moons orbit one way. The other one orbits the other way!

Prove It

What are some details that show that people couldn't live on the solar system's other planets?

207

The Moon

by Iris Dao

The Moon is our closest neighbor in space. It orbits around our planet. The Moon takes about 29 days to circle Earth.

The Moon does not make its own light. It just reflects light from the Sun. We can see the Moon because the Sun shines on it.

As the Moon orbits Earth, the Sun shines on different parts of it. So the Moon reflects different amounts of light. That's why the Moon's shape seems to change.

We call these changes the **phases** of the Moon. The first phase is the new moon. We can't see the Moon at all during this phase. That's because the Sun is shining only on the part of the Moon facing away from Earth.

As the Moon slowly turns to face Earth, we start to see it again. Each day, the Moon reflects more light. First we see a crescent moon, then a half-moon. After about fourteen days, a full moon shines at night. These phases of the Moon happen every month in the same order.

After the full moon, the Moon reflects less and less light to Earth. So it seems to get smaller. The Moon changes to a half-moon and then a crescent moon. Then it becomes a new moon, and the cycle starts over.

Long ago, people noticed the regular pattern of the Moon's phases. They used it to keep track of time. In fact, our word *month* comes from *Moon*!

Grace Blasts Off

in *Starring Grace* by Mary Hoffman

Grace lives with her mother and Nana, her grandmother. Nana is away visiting a friend in Texas. While Nana is gone, Grace stays with her friend Aimee's mom until her own mother gets home from work.

Nana had been gone for over a week when Aimee's mom brought Grace home and Grace found an envelope with a beautiful stamp on it on the mat. The envelope had blue flowers and a Texas postmark.

"Nana!" thought Grace. But the letter was addressed to Ma.

As soon as Ma opened the door, Grace met her with a cup of tea and her slippers.

"Sit down, sit down, Ma," she said excitedly. "Here's your tea. And here's a letter from Nana! Open it and read it to me, please!"

"All right, all right," said Ma. "Let me get my breath." But she did open the letter. "Look, here's one inside just for you," she said. "And a photo. Oh, my! What *has* Nana done?"

Grace took the photo. And there was Nana's lovely familiar face, but she was dressed as an astronaut! Grace's eyes got bigger and bigger. "Nana hasn't gone up in space, has she?" she asked.

Ma laughed until the tears ran down her cheeks.

"Oh, honey, you should see your face! I don't think so, but let's read our letters and find out."

Grace's letter was hard to read. She wasn't used to reading Nana's handwriting. But what it said was very exciting. Nana had been to the NASA Space Center and seen Mission Control and eaten special space ice cream. And then she had her photo taken in a studio that made her look like an astronaut.

"Well, doesn't that beat everything!" said Ma. "My mother, the astronaut. I know that some older people are going up in space now, but I never thought I'd see your nana dressed up in a space suit and helmet."

Grace's eyes were shining. She had never thought of being an astronaut, but now her imagination was working overtime.

"Do you know any stories about space, Ma?" she asked.

"Well, I can tell you about the night I stayed up to watch the first people walk on the Moon," said Ma. "In fact, why don't we go out and get Chinese food tonight and I'll tell you over dinner? I'm getting sick of my own cooking."

It was the best night since Nana had left. They had chow mein and fried rice and spring rolls and pancakes with a spicy sauce, and Grace ate as much as she possibly could. So did Ma, and she told Grace about when she was a little girl, much younger than Grace was now, and they had seen the first people on the Moon.

Zoom In

What caused Grace and Ma to start talking about the first people on the Moon? What evidence did you use?

"We didn't have our own TV then—imagine!—so we went to a neighbor's house. In fact, it was Coralita's house, you know, the friend Nana is staying with now. There were about a dozen kids crammed on the sofa, all very sleepy because it was way past our bedtime, and then the landing was delayed, so it got even later. I kept dozing off and then your nana shook me awake and said, 'Look, look, Ava, that's the Moon and that man coming down the ladder will be the first person to step on it.' I couldn't believe it. I mean, it was all just like a dusty old desert, not a bit like the shiny, silvery Moon Nana used to take me out to see on clear nights."

Maybe Ma didn't tell the story as well as Nana would have done, but it was a story all the same and Grace was fascinated by it. Over the weekend she borrowed all the space books she could find in the library and played astronauts with the gang. She showed them the photo and told them that Nana was going into space.

"I'm Mae Jemison," said Grace, "and I'm launching my shuttle. Ten . . . nine . . . eight . . . seven . . . six . . . five . . . four . . . three . . . two . . . one—BLAST OFF!"

And she ran around the backyard with her arms out wide, flapping them so hard, she nearly did take off. Aimee and Raj and Kester and Maria were at Grace's house, and there was only one game they wanted to play. They pretended there was no gravity by walking slowly around the yard, taking huge steps, and bouncing slowly up and down.

"I'm going to be an astronaut when I grow up," said Grace.

"So am I," said Kester. "It's the best job. You get to be weightless and eat dried food, so you don't have to wash the dishes."

"Me, too," said the others.

"But we can't be astronauts without a spaceship," said Grace. "Let's build one!"

So they found a lot of cardboard boxes and some crates that Nana's marmalade oranges had come in, and tied them together with string. It didn't look very much like a spaceship when they had finished, but two small astronauts could just about squeeze into the "capsule" at the same time. They took turns.

But blasting off was difficult; the spaceship always toppled over.

"I know," said Grace. "Let's prop it up against a tree so it's upright."

It was Grace's turn to be captain. Aimee was her navigator and the others were Mission Control. It was much more difficult to get into the spaceship now that it was propped against the tree.

"Okay," said Raj. "All systems are go. Prepare for liftoff. Ten . . . nine . . . eight . . ."

By the time he got to three, the spaceship was wobbling alarmingly. Aimee was trying to make herself more comfortable in the crate and Grace was trying to keep it steady. When Raj reached BLAST OFF! the whole contraption collapsed and Grace and Aimee fell into a heap.

Zoom In

Why do the children need boxes and crates? What part of the story helped you answer?

"Ow!" yelled Aimee. "You're sitting on my hand. It really hurts."

Grace had a bump on her head that was growing before their eyes. But Aimee was clutching her wrist with her other hand and her face had gotten very white. Hearing the noise, Ma came running out into the yard. She took one look at the astronauts and sent Mission Control home. Then she called Aimee's mom and they took the two girls to the doctor.

Grace was given a big bandage on her forehead and Aimee had her arm put in a sling.

"It's all right," said the doctor. "It's not broken. Just a sprain. And Grace is going to be fine."

"What on earth were you doing?" asked Ma on the way home.

"We were launching into space," said Grace. "Only our spaceship fell over."

"It was fantastic," Aimee added happily. Her wrist was throbbing, but she didn't mind.

"It's a well-known fact that space travel is dangerous," Ma told them. "So I'm going to say right now—and I think Aimee's mom will agree with me—that there are to be no more astronaut games."

"Absolutely," agreed Aimee's mom. "These space explorers are grounded."

"That's okay," said Grace. "We don't want to play astronauts anymore. I want to be a doctor now!"

Prove It

What is Grace like? Use details from the story to help you describe the way she thinks and behaves.

The Sun and the Stars

by Moussa Mpenza

The Sun

The Sun gives us light and heat. Without those things, there would be no life on Earth.

The Sun is about 100 times larger than Earth. Because the Sun is so big, its **gravity** is strong enough to keep all the planets in orbit.

About three-quarters of the Sun is made up of hydrogen. Another gas, helium, makes up most of the rest. Deep inside the Sun, the temperature is more than 15 million degrees Celsius!

The high temperature deep inside the Sun causes a reaction. The hydrogen there changes into helium. This gives off tremendous heat and light.

The heat and light travel up to the Sun's surface and out into space. It takes a little over eight minutes for the light and heat to reach Earth. The other planets in our solar system get light from the Sun, too.

▲ Huge flames on the Sun can be 100,000 miles high.

The Stars

Without a telescope, you can see about 3,000 stars in the sky at night. There are many more stars out there though. Scientists think that there may be 1,000,000,000,000,000,000,000,000 stars in the universe.

Our Sun is just one of those stars. Because it's the star closest to Earth, it looks bigger and brighter than all the others. It's not though.

Many stars are much larger than the Sun. Some are a thousand times wider than the Sun.

Like the Sun, the other stars in the sky are huge balls of gas. They give off light and heat. Many stars have planets orbiting them, just as the Sun does.

Long ago, people spent a lot of time watching the sky. They saw patterns in the stars. One group of stars looked like a bear, for example. Another group looked like a hunter.

Today we call these patterns constellations. In all, there are 88 constellations. Astronomers use them for mapping the stars.

Zoom In

Why does our Sun appear bigger and brighter than other stars?

The Milky Way

Most stars are found in large groups called galaxies. There are millions of galaxies in the universe. The Sun and Earth are in a galaxy called the Milky Way.

Our galaxy is shaped like a spiral with a bulge in the middle. The Sun is at the edge of one of the arms of the spiral.

The Milky Way has over 200 billion stars of its own. That sounds huge, but our galaxy is actually medium-sized. The largest known galaxy has over 100 trillion stars. Small galaxies have about 10 billion stars.

You are here.

The Universe

How big is the universe? Some people say that it never ends. That is very difficult for us to understand. Suppose the universe does have an edge. What is beyond the edge? That is not any easier to understand!

Scientists measure huge distances in light-years. One light-year is nearly six million million miles. We know that the universe is *at least* 28 billion light-years across! It could be far bigger. We do not know, but some day we might just find out.

Prove It

What details do you learn about our galaxy from the text and pictures?

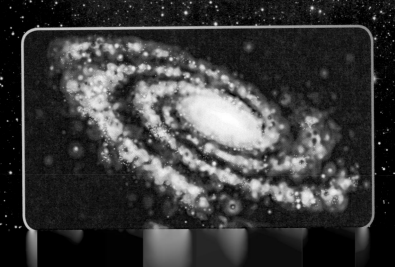

Learn the Words

gravity
train
weightless
crew
experience
space shuttle

- Read the words on the list.
- Read the dialogue.
- Find the words.

I wonder if the **space shuttle** is flying up there right now.

1. Tell What It's Like
Writing

Pretend you are one of the people in the picture. Write a paragraph. Tell where you are in the picture. Describe what you see up in the sky. Describe how it makes you feel. Show your paragraph to your partner.

2. You Are the Actor
Listening and Speaking

Work with a partner. Take turns reading the dialogue in the picture. Ask your partner about any words you don't understand. When you read, use your best acting voice. Make the dialogue come alive.

3. Take a Survey
Graphic Organizer

Ask at least five classmates where they want to go in space. Tally their votes. Share your findings with your partner.

Where Do You Want to Go in Space?	
the Moon	the Space Shuttle

4. You're on TV!
Listening and Speaking

You will talk to an astronaut on TV. You are going to ask about life on the space shuttle. Think of five questions to ask about the shuttle. Ask your partner your questions. Listen to your partner's questions. Ask your partner about any words you don't understand.

TRAVELING THROUGH SPACE

by Marc Rodo

The closest object in outer space is the Moon. It is still a very long trip, though. Getting to the Moon is not easy. In fact, only twelve people have actually been on the Moon.

The rocket Apollo 11 carried the first astronauts to the Moon. Neil Armstrong stepped onto the Moon's surface. People at home actually watched the Moon landing on their televisions!

▲ Neil Armstrong, the first man on the Moon

The twelve people who visited the Moon were not the only ones to explore in outer space. There have been almost 500 astronauts in space. The astronauts come from different countries.

Most of these astronauts have been crew members on a **space shuttle**. There are usually between five and seven astronauts on each space shuttle.

A space shuttle flies about 200 miles above Earth. The astronauts feel weightless. They feel as though they are floating.

Sometimes astronauts go on spacewalks. They do this so they can work outside the spacecraft. Sometimes they need to do an experiment. Sometimes the astronauts need to fix something. Can you imagine floating through space?

▲ An astronaut outside the space shuttle

Space probes without people aboard have flown even more amazing distances. The Voyager space probes explore the solar system. One of the probes is now 10 billion miles from Earth!

Another spacecraft without people on it looks like a car. It is exploring the surface of Mars. It is trying to find out whether Mars has ever had life on it. The probe's name is a very good one. It is called *Curiosity*.

Prove It

What details tell you that people on Earth have found more than one way to explore space?

Retell "The Sun and the Stars"

 When you retell a selection, you tell only the main ideas and important details. This will help readers understand the selection.

"The Sun and the Stars" is nonfiction. It gives facts about the universe. Review the selection on pages 220–225. Look at the pictures on page 233.

■ **First Picture:** What is special about our Sun? Why is it important to Earth?

■ **The Other Three Pictures:** What are the main ideas of the other sections? What important details did you learn about outer space in each one?

Use the pictures on page 233 to retell the selection to your partner. As you talk about each fact or example, point to the correct picture. Use complete sentences.

Words you might use in your retelling:	
solar system	planet
outer space	gravity

in outer space

the Sun

the universe

the stars

the Milky Way

Dig Deeper

Look Back

Here are two facts about outer space from this unit.

■ Many stars are much larger than the Sun.

■ The planet Saturn has bright rings around it.

Work with a partner. Look back through this unit. Find the selection that gives each fact. Use heads and other text features to help you look.

Take turns. One partner should work alone to find a fact from the unit. The other partner should hunt to see where this fact came from. Then switch tasks with your partner.

Talk About It

The Sun is hot.

The Sun is hot and bright.

The Sun is hot and bright and yellow.

The Sun is hot and bright and yellow and huge.

The Sun is hot and bright and yellow and huge and fiery.

Now it's your turn. Work with your classmates to describe Earth. Keep adding details.

Conversation

To speak formally, use more polite words. Use a different tone of voice. You might show less feeling than normal. You might make your voice lower. You might speak more slowly.

Talk to a partner. One of you will be person A. The other will be person B.

Person A

Use **formal** language. Tell your partner about an event.

Reply in formal language.

Reply in informal language. Ask how your partner feels about the event.

Person B

Reply in formal language. Ask how your partner feels about the event.

Use **informal** language to tell about the same event.

Reply in informal language.

Our Valuable
EARTH

The **BIG** Question

What can we do to help our planet?

☐ Why do you think our animals, our forests, and our oceans need to be protected from pollution?

☐ How can we protect our precious natural resources?

☐ Why is it important to recycle?

How can people pollute less and waste less?

1. What are some natural resources we use?

We use...

- ☐ oil.
- ☐ wood.
- ☐ water.
- ☐ metal.

2. What can we recycle?

We can recycle...

- ☐ paper.
- ☐ cans.
- ☐ plastic.
- ☐ glass.

3. Why is too much garbage bad?

Too much garbage...

- ☐ wastes natural resources.
- ☐ pollutes water and land.
- ☐ can harm plants, animals, and people.

4. How can we make less garbage?

We can...

- ☐ use less.
- ☐ recycle more.
- ☐ clean up litter.

Say **more!**

Learn the Words

natural resources

energy

oil

pollute

conserve

careless

Theme Vocabulary

ⓘ The easiest way to remember the meaning of a new word is to use the word. As you discuss natural resources, use these vocabulary words. Use them when you read and write about natural resources, too.

Read the word.

Look at the picture.

Listen to your teacher.

natural resources

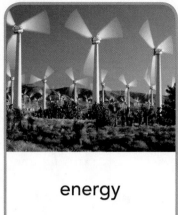

energy

oil

pollute

conserve

careless

How Do You Feel?

Look at the vocabulary cards. Choose one picture and tell how it makes you feel.

Pablo and Pedro are my twin brothers.

They may look the same, but they are very different.

1

Pablo is very good at basketball.

Pedro can't keep up.

2

Pedro has a great swing.

Pablo is not so good at baseball.

3

Pablo is a math whiz. Pedro can't multiply to save his life.

4

242 Graphic Novel

Pedro loves to read. Books put Pablo to sleep.

5

This week, the whole school took a big test.

Math in the morning, reading in the afternoon.

6

Pablo took the test on Monday in Miss Clay's class.

7

Pedro took it on Tuesday in Miss Clark's class.

8

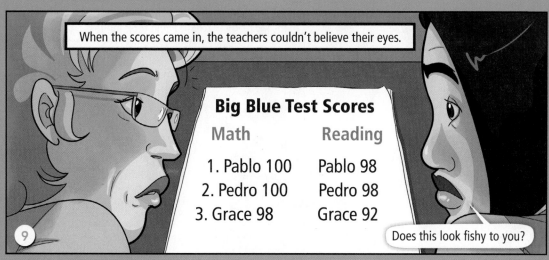

When the scores came in, the teachers couldn't believe their eyes.

Big Blue Test Scores

Math	Reading
1. Pablo 100	Pablo 98
2. Pedro 100	Pedro 98
3. Grace 98	Grace 92

9

Does this look fishy to you?

4 Formal/Informal Language To be a "math whiz" means to be "very good at math." Is this expression formal language or informal language?

243

Pedro, did you take the reading test for Pablo on Monday afternoon?

No way!

That is hard to believe. Pablo never does so well at reading.

10

Pedro's math score is fishy. Did you take the test for him on Tuesday morning, Pablo?

Ask Marta. She is in the class, too.

11

Did Pablo take the test for Pedro on Tuesday morning?

12

It's hard to say. But if you want to be sure, why not give them the test at the same time?

13

So the next day, Pedro and Pablo took the test again.

14

⑩ **Formal/Informal Language** When the teacher asks Pedro if he took the reading test for Pablo, Pedro answers informally, "No way!" How could he say "No way!" in a more formal way?

244

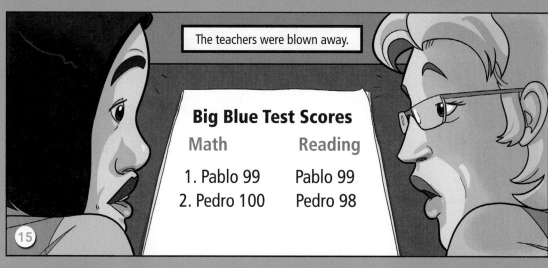

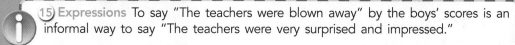

15 **Expressions** To say "The teachers were blown away" by the boys' scores is an informal way to say "The teachers were very surprised and impressed."

245

Natural Resources

Some **natural resources** don't get used up.

Sunlight
We need sunlight for heat and light. It is Earth's main source of **energy**. We use sunlight today, but that doesn't mean there will be less sunlight tomorrow.

Water
Water falls from clouds. It flows in rivers. It reaches the ocean. It forms clouds. It falls from clouds again. In a way, water **recycles** itself!

Wood
We use wood to make houses, chairs, pencils, and a lot more. We cut down trees, but we can plant new ones. If we **conserve** our forests, we will have enough wood.

Some natural resources do get used up. If we use them in a **careless** way, we will run out of them.

Oil

The world uses 85 million barrels of **oil** a day. It takes millions of years for oil to form. Each barrel we use is a barrel that is gone forever.

Coal

Like oil, coal is an important source of energy. Coal takes millions of years to form, too. When we burn coal, it goes up in smoke.

Uranium

Uranium is a metal that is used to make nuclear power. There's only so much uranium on Earth. Once it's gone, it can never be replaced.

Say "No!" to Plastic

by Derek Chavez

When I visit my grandmother, I always go with her to the grocery store. At the checkout counter, the clerks used to ask, "Paper or plastic?" But now they just pack everything in plastic bags. Why?

Plastic bags are cheap. If it's raining or snowing, they don't fall apart the way paper bags do. But when we throw plastic bags away, we cause big problems to the environment.

Plastic bags get into the oceans, where they kill birds and sea animals.

They clutter up landfills. They clog drains. It takes hundreds of years for plastic to decompose.

There are things we can and must do. First, we need laws to stop stores from using plastic bags.

Second, every family should have three or four sturdy, reusable bags. They should take these bags along whenever they go shopping, and use them instead of plastic.

Why should we care?

We have to make sure our planet doesn't become a giant garbage dump in the future.

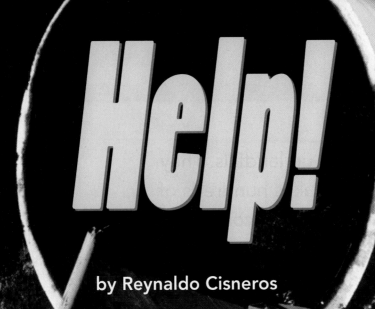

Help!

by Reynaldo Cisneros

Look at that chimney—all that smoke,
The air around is airless!
It's so bad all the trees will choke.
How can we be so careless?

Look at the mess dumped in the **creek**.
There's no point going fishing.
It's getting worse here, week by week.
It won't be cured by wishing.

Look at the trash by the side of the road,
At the dead crops on the farm.
It hasn't rained or even snowed.
Someone pull the earth alarm!

Hurt No Living Thing

by Christina Rossetti

Hurt no living thing:
Ladybird, nor butterfly,
Nor moth with dusty wing,
Nor cricket chirping cheerily,
Nor grasshopper so light of leap,
Nor dancing gnat, nor beetle fat,
Nor harmless worms that creep.

The Life of a CAN

by Ross Eliot

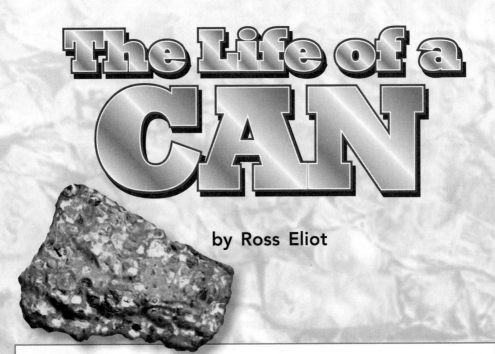

Pop the top of your favorite drink. Then ask yourself two questions. Where did that aluminum can come from? Where will it go?

The ore that contains aluminum is called bauxite. It lies deep in the ground. Giant machines dig it out.

Trucks carry the bauxite ore to a factory. There the aluminum is removed from the ore. From two tons of ore, the factory makes one ton of aluminum.

Getting aluminum from the ore takes a great deal of energy. Smoke and **chemicals** from the plant can **pollute** the air.

Some of the aluminum is rolled into thin sheets. Those sheets go to a can factory. Aluminum can factories turn out millions of cans each year.

The new cans go to another factory. There the cans are filled with your favorite drinks. Finally, tops are sealed onto the cans.

After you finish your favorite drink, what do you do with the empty can? It would be careless to throw it in the **garbage**. Empty cans are easy to recycle.

Today, more than half of all aluminum cans are recycled. Lots of other aluminum items are recycled, too.

Recycled cans get melted down and rolled into aluminum sheets again. That saves a lot of energy. Recycling aluminum takes much less energy than making new aluminum from bauxite.

Recycling aluminum also conserves natural resources. It lets us leave bauxite in the ground for the future. Recycling also reduces the gases that pollute the air.

More than half of the aluminum we use today comes from recycling. Recycling is also fast. Recycle an aluminum can today. In less than two months the aluminum will be back in a brand new can. Ready to use and then recycle again!

factory

recycling

recycling factory

ore

Prove It

What details show that recycling cans helps to conserve natural resources?

255

ALL THINGS ARE LINKED

adapted from an African folktale
retold by Pierre Dulac

The Chief ruled the whole village. He liked to give orders to his people. He gave a lot of orders.

Sometimes the Chief's orders were cruel. That didn't matter to him. Cruel or not, his people always followed his orders. They were afraid not to. That's what people do sometimes.

One night, the Chief had trouble sleeping. The frogs in the creek were making too much noise. The next morning he gave an order. "Kill all the frogs in the creek!" he told his people.

The people didn't want to **harm** the frogs. They were afraid of the Chief, though. So they followed the order. By the end of the day, all the frogs were dead.

The Chief's Grandmother shook her head. "Killing the frogs was a mistake," she told the Chief.

"The frogs made too much noise," he said. "Now it is nice and quiet here."

"Those frogs had important work to do," said Grandmother. "Don't you know that all things are linked?"

The Chief laughed. "Frogs don't work," he said. "And I am not linked with the frogs!"

The Chief slept soundly that night. Grandmother didn't. She knew the silence was not a good thing.

A few nights later, the Chief couldn't sleep again. This time, a loud buzzing filled his house. Mosquitoes were everywhere!

The mosquitoes bit the Chief's nose and toes. He slapped at the mosquitoes, but he couldn't get rid of them. In the morning, he was covered with bites.

The Chief called his people together. "Go to the creek and kill every mosquito," he ordered.

The people knew they could not kill all the mosquitoes. There were too many of them. Even so, they tried to follow the Chief's order. That's what people do sometimes.

Everyone in the village spent the day killing mosquitoes. People waded up and down the creek, slapping. They walked through the woods, swatting. They worked in the fields, smacking.

It was no use. More and more mosquitoes were hatching all the time. By late afternoon, there were more mosquitoes than ever.

That night, the Chief was furious. Swarms of mosquitoes still buzzed around his house. "I gave my people an order," he shouted. "Why haven't they followed it?"

Zoom In

What details show that the Chief has made a bad decision about the frogs?

259

Grandmother looked over at the Chief. "How can a hundred people kill so many mosquitoes? What did you expect?"

"I expect the people to follow orders!" shouted the Chief.

Grandmother shook her head. "Mosquitoes lay millions of eggs," she said. "Usually the frogs eat most of the eggs. Now the frogs are gone. So all the mosquito eggs are hatching. Remember, all things are linked."

The Chief swatted a mosquito that had just bitten his nose. "I am not linked with mosquitoes," he said.

The Chief called the people together again. "Today you will kill all the mosquitoes— or else!" he said.

"This is crazy. I want to live near a creek with frogs," one villager said. "I don't want to kill mosquitoes."

"Let's move," someone whispered.

And that's just what they did. Secretly, the villagers packed up their things and left the village. Up in his hut, the Chief didn't even know they had left.

The people walked and walked through the forest. In time, they came to a creek filled with frogs. Hardly any mosquitoes buzzed around. So they built a new village there.

That's what people do sometimes.

Prove It

What did the Chief's grandmother mean when she said that all things are linked?

261

The Farmer's Sons

BASED ON A FABLE BY AESOP

— CAST OF CHARACTERS —
NARRATOR, FARMER, SON 1, SON 2, SON 3

Scene 1

Setting: Long ago on a family's farm. All the characters are onstage.

NARRATOR: An old farmer had worked his land for many years. He had three sons, but they had never helped him very much on the farm.

FARMER: Sons, you know I will not live forever. Somewhere on this farm is hidden a great treasure. If you look hard enough, you'll find it. When you do, you'll have all you need.

SONS 1, 2, and 3 (*together*): We will! We promise!

NARRATOR: The old farmer soon passed away, and the sons seemed to forget their promise.

(*As the* NARRATOR *speaks, the* FARMER *gets up and leaves the stage.*)

SON 1 (*excitedly*): Look! Dad left a bag of coins. There's enough for us all to buy new clothes. Let's go shopping.

SON 2: No need to plant a crop this year. Dad filled the barn with wheat last fall. We'll have enough bread for months.

SON 3: I think I'll make chicken for dinner again. There are still hens in the chicken coop.

NARRATOR: As the months passed, the three careless sons used up what their father had left. Before long, all they had was their land.

SON 1: I'm hungry. And there's no more money or food. What are we going to do?

SON 2: Didn't Dad say there was a treasure buried on the farm? We should dig for it.

NARRATOR: So the three sons got shovels and went into the fields to dig.

(Behind the NARRATOR, the SONS go into the field with shovels and start digging.)

SON 1: We've dug up this whole field twice. And we haven't found a penny.

SON 2: Let's clear away those rocks. Maybe the treasure is under them.

SON 3: We should also dig up those weeds.

Prove It

What do the sons learn in Scene 2? Which character's words helped you to know?

Scene 2

Setting: The next spring. The SONS *and the* NARRATOR *are onstage.*

NARRATOR: The sons dug every inch of land. Still they found no treasure. The fields looked great, though.

SON 1: Maybe we should plant crops.

NARRATOR: That's what the sons did. All their digging had prepared the soil. So their crops grew well.

SON 2 *(counting money)*: Our vegetables sell fast at the market. Look how much we earned.

SON 3: There really was a treasure in this land. And by working hard, we found it.

SAVING ENERGY

by Malika Sterling

There's no place like home for saving energy. Take a short tour around a house and see. There are many ways to save electricity, gas, and oil.

Let's start in the kitchen. The refrigerator uses a lot of electricity to stay cool. Don't leave the door open any longer than you have to. If you do, the refrigerator uses more energy.

This kitchen has an oven and a microwave. The microwave uses less energy to cook. Whenever possible, try to use it.

Let's move on to the laundry room. Before you leave the kitchen, or any room, turn off the lights.

Did you know you can use cold water in a washing machine? Cold water gets the clothes just as clean. By not heating the water, you save energy.

The clothes dryer is always handy. It needs a lot of energy to do its work. That's why some people use clotheslines. Outside, the sun will dry your clothes for free. An inside clothes rack also works.

Everyone spends a lot of time in the living room. People use a lot of energy there, too.

The thermostat is on the living room wall. It's set at 72 degrees this winter. It could be turned down to 68. That would save a lot of energy. It would save oil, gas, or electricity.

There's no one in the living room, but the TV is on. Someone got careless and forgot to turn it off.

It's the middle of the day, and a living room lamp is on. The curtains are closed, though. Open the curtains, and turn off the lamp. Sunlight is free!

Zoom In

What details tell you how turning down the thermostat can help you conserve?

The bathroom is a place to save energy, too. There's a bathtub and a shower. Which uses less hot water and energy? Showers, if they're short enough, are the better choice.

You don't have to leave the water running while you brush your teeth. You can conserve water by turning it off while you brush.

This sink faucet leaks a bit. Fixing it would save a lot of money. Each week, **gallons** of hot water are going down the drain.

There's also a water heater in this bathroom. It's set at 150 degrees. The temperature could be turned down to 120. The water will still be hot enough.

In the bedroom, the computer is on. A lot of people leave computers on at night. Make a point of turning yours off. The same goes for music and video game players. It won't harm them, and it will save resources.

The desk in this bedroom is next to a sunny window. That's a good idea. The sun, not an electric bulb, lights up the desk.

Cold air is leaking through this window. A room loses a lot of heat that way. Sealing small leaks saves a lot of energy!

We're through in here. Let's go outside and find some ways to save energy there.

The car on the driveway is idling, but no one is inside. That's a waste of oil. It also pollutes the air. Ask your parents to turn off the car when they're not driving it.

Here's another idea. See that bicycle in the garage? Use it for short trips. Then your parents won't have to use the car as much.

Carpools save energy, too. Try riding in one car with your friends to school or sports. Carpooling can be a lot of fun.

Look around your house. What are some ways you can save energy? The more you save, the better off you'll be.

Prove It

Use details from the text to say how you would tell a friend the best ways to save energy.

Learn the Words

creek

gallon

recycle

garbage

chemical

harm

- Read the words on the list.
- Read the dialogue.
- Find the words.

Put all **garbage** in this bin. Don't throw bottles and cans here, though!

GARBAGE BIN

1. Give a Speech
Listening and Speaking

Pretend you are a character from the picture above. Prepare a speech about recycling. Tell why it is important. Work on your speech with your partner. You can look at selections from this unit for information. Give your speech to the class.

2. Make a Chart
Graphic Organizer

Work with your partner. Think about items you can recycle. What items belong in each category? See how many you and your partner can name. Ask your partner about any words you don't understand.

metal	
plastic	
glass	

3. Use It Again
Listening and Speaking

Think of a way to turn a bottle, can, newspaper, or plastic item into something useful. Draw a picture of what you can make. Share your picture with your partner. Tell how to make the item.

4. Write a Poem
Writing

What would an animal tell us about saving natural resources? Choose an animal. Think how the animal would talk about this. Write the animal's words as a poem. Use the poem "Help!" in this unit as a model. Your poem doesn't have to rhyme. Show your poem to your partner.

What Have We Here?

by Rosa Goodman

Each part of nature plays a role in keeping the planet healthy. Small changes in one part of nature can affect the rest in unexpected ways.

Animals

Earth has a huge variety of animals. Some animals are in danger though. When one kind of animal dies out, it has an effect on other parts of nature.

Blackfooted ferrets, for example, were once common on the prairies. They ate small prairie dogs. Early settlers, however, poisoned the prairie dogs. As a result, the ferrets had no food. Today, blackfooted ferrets are the rarest mammal in North America.

Forests

Today, many forests are being cut down and cleared. That has a big effect on nature.

The animals that lived in these forests often die. So do the plants.

Without trees, soil tends to wash away, or erode. It clogs and dirties nearby creeks and rivers. As a result, cities downstream have less clean water.

Trees and plants are important for another reason. They use carbon dioxide to make oxygen. Without forests, there is more carbon dioxide in the air. That causes temperatures around the globe to rise.

Oceans

Rising temperatures cause problems in the ocean. Tiny sea animals called krill die off when the water gets too warm.

Many fish feed on krill. Without krill, the number of fish goes down. Today the fish population in the ocean is at a dangerous low.

With fewer fish, there's less food for ocean birds. Whales, seals, and other ocean mammals have less to eat. So their numbers fall, too.

People also like to eat fish. Today, however, this food is less available to us.

Climate

Over time, warming temperatures can change climates.

In the Arctic, the climate is getting warmer. More and more ice is melting. That raises the level of the sea.

Many large cities are near the ocean. If all the Arctic ice melts, some cities may be flooded.

Higher temperatures and the loss of trees can make the climate much drier. Some parts of Africa, for example, are becoming deserts. There is no longer enough rain to grow crops. To survive, people and animals must move.

Prove It

How did the author organize this selection? What evidence did you use?

Retell "All Things Are Linked"

 When you retell a selection, you tell only the main ideas and important details. This will help readers understand the selection.

"All Things Are Linked" is a folktale about the Chief, who always wants things done his way. Review the story on pages 256–261. Look at the pictures on page 279.

■ Beginning: What did the Chief tell the people to do about the frogs? What did the people do?

■ Middle: What happened next? What did the Chief order because of it? What did the people try to do?

■ End: What did the Chief order at the end? What did the people do this time?

Use the pictures on page 279 to retell the selection to your partner. As you tell about the Chief's actions and their effects, point to the correct picture. Use complete sentences.

Words you might use in your retelling:	
creek	careless
conserve	harm

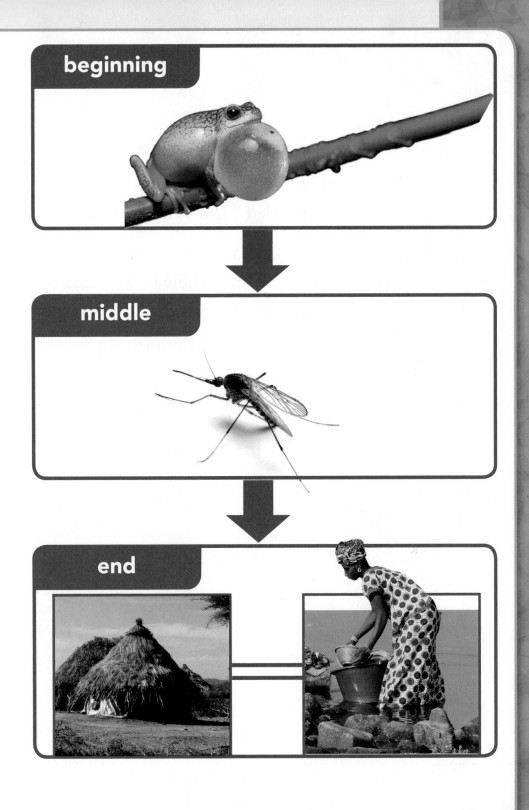

beginning

middle

end

Dig Deeper

Look Back

Look back at the play "The Farmer's Sons." Suppose you and a partner are writing an online review of this play. Your review will be titled "The Wise Father."

Work with your partner. Talk about what the father is like in the play. How does Scene 2 show how wise he really was? What details does the author use to show this? Work with your partner to write all this in your review, "The Wise Father."

Talk About It

How can we combine two sentences?

He turned off the light. Turning off lights saves energy.

He turned off the light **because** turning off lights saves energy.

Work with a partner. Come up with two sentences that can be combined using the word *because*.

Conversation

> When people **negotiate**, they try to find a solution. They listen to each other. They find what each person wants. They try to come to an agreement that helps both people.

Talk to a partner. One of you will be person A. The other will be person B.

Person A   **Person B**

Suggest how you and your partner can share one computer.

→ Reply. Disagree. Suggest another way to share it.

Reply. Explain why your solution is better.

→ Reply. Tell why your solution is better.

Agree with your partner.

→ Tell what you have both agreed to do.

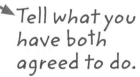

★ ★ ★ ★ **We the** ★ ★ ★ ★ ★
★ ★ **People** ★ ★

The **BIG** Question

How can we be good citizens?

☐ What are some things people can do to help their community?

☐ What community groups do you know about?

☐ Who are some of the people in our government?

1. How can people be responsible?

Responsible people…

- ☐ obey the laws.
- ☐ drive carefully.
- ☐ put trash in garbage cans.
- ☐ help others.

2. What can a community be?

A community can be…

- ☐ a city block.
- ☐ a neighborhood.
- ☐ a town.
- ☐ a group of farms.

3. What problems can a community have?

A community can have problems with...

☐ traffic.

☐ housing.

☐ garbage.

4. What solutions can a community find for its problems?

A community can...

☐ add traffic lights and signs.

☐ send out garbage trucks more often.

☐ ask people to be more responsible.

ONE WAY

Say **more!**

Learn the Words

citizen
vote
election
campaign
community
responsible

Theme Vocabulary

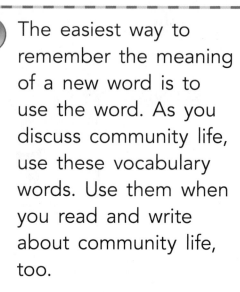 The easiest way to remember the meaning of a new word is to use the word. As you discuss community life, use these vocabulary words. Use them when you read and write about community life, too.

Read the word.
Look at the picture.
Listen to your teacher.

citizen

vote

election

campaign

community

responsible

Which Picture?

Look at the vocabulary cards. Choose one picture.
Don't tell anyone what it is! Describe the picture.
See if your partner can guess which picture you chose.

6 You got her!

Here you go. But watch out! She's a little grumpy.

7 RRRiPPP!!

Oh no!

8 I have a hole in my pants!

9 No time to go home. I hope my coat will hide it.

Thanks!

10 You're late, Chad. What happened?

Jane Rand.

Sorry, Mrs. Rand. I was giving my friend a hand.

 10 **Expressions** To "give someone a hand" is an informal way of saying "to help someone."

289

 13 Formal/Informal Language When Mrs. Rand says, "Would you please take your coat off," is she using formal or informal language? How can you tell?

290

Detention Hall

 (17) **Formal/Informal Language** Chad uses formal language when he talks to Mr. Wild. Describe a situation in which he might use informal language.

291

Our NATION'S CAPITAL

by Mary Vega

Washington, DC, is the capital of the United States. It is the center of our nation's government.

Washington, DC, is located between Maryland and Virginia. The city is called the District of Columbia. Washington, DC, is not a state. It is not part of another state either.

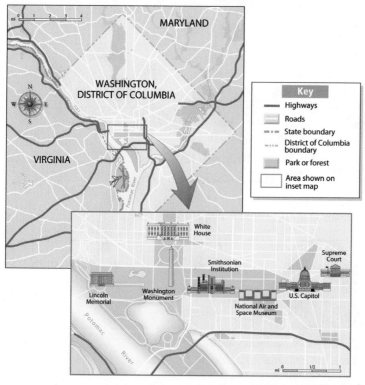

▲ The government buildings are in Washington, DC.

The White House is in Washington, DC. The President lives in the White House and works in the Oval Office there.

Down the street from the White House is the U.S. Capitol. This is where members of Congress discuss the country's **problems**. They work to come up with the right **solutions**.

Government buildings, such as the Capitol, are in Washington, DC. ▼

The Truth About Aloha

by Marissa Feliciano

Friday was oral report day in Kevin's classroom. Kevin decided to talk about his relative. Aloha Vivartes was an American pioneer, and he was Kevin's ancestor. After he finished his report, the class gave Kevin a big round of applause. He was smiling until he noticed that his teacher was frowning at him.

"Kevin," she said. "The assignment was to report on a real person in America's history."

Kevin stared at his shoes. "Aloha is real. He is my relative," he said. Ms. Marsh shook her head but said nothing.

After school, as Kevin neared his house, he could see his father sitting on the front porch. "Tell me the real story about our famous relative," Kevin said.

"That was a just a story," said his dad, chuckling. "My father made him up, and I'm carrying on the family tradition."

"Great," Kevin said. "I have made an idiot of myself."

The next day, Kevin asked Ms. Marsh's permission to address the class. "I learned something important yesterday," he said. "First, I learned that my true family story was not true at all. Second, I learned that I come from a long line of storytellers. In fact, I know that storytelling is in my blood. And that is not a bad thing."

His class cheered again. Kevin sat down with a big smile on his face.

A Citizen

by Eva Sánchez

Lourdes was born in Cuba. She came to the United States when she was twelve. For a long time, she wanted to become a **citizen** of the United States. As a citizen, she would have more opportunities and freedoms.

A U.S. citizen has rights and privileges. The government protects its citizens. In return, citizens have a duty to support the leaders of their **community** and country.

Anyone born in the United States is an American citizen automatically. For immigrants, like Lourdes, becoming a citizen is more difficult.

of the United States

When Lourdes was eighteen years old, she decided that it was time to become a citizen.

Before applying, immigrants must live in the United States for five years. Lourdes had lived here for six years. She had a Permanent Resident Card. That shows Lourdes came to this country legally.

Lourdes filled out a form for citizenship. Then she went for an interview with a government official. The official asked her questions about her job, her home, and other activities.

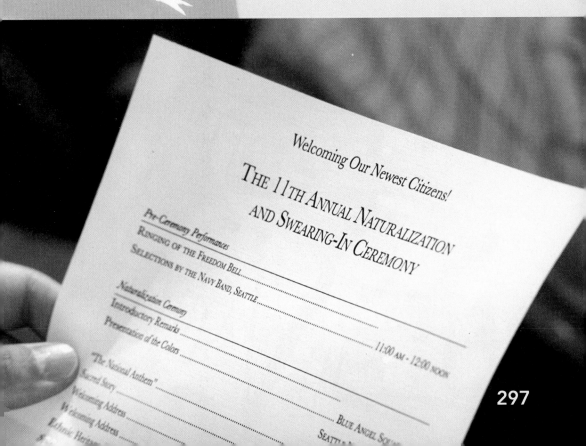

Welcoming Our Newest Citizens!

THE 11TH ANNUAL NATURALIZATION AND SWEARING-IN CEREMONY

Pre-Ceremony Performances
RINGING OF THE FREEDOM BELL.................................
SELECTIONS BY THE NAVY BAND, SEATTLE.....................

Naturalization Ceremony
Introductory Remarks.................................
Presentation of the Colors.................................
                                        11:00 AM - 12:00 NOON
"The National Anthem".................................
Sacred Story.................................
Welcoming Address.................................
Welcoming Address .... BLUE ANGEL SQ...
Ethnic Heritage.................................   SEATTL...

Part of the interview was a test. Immigrants need to read and write English. They need to know about American history and government. Lourdes learned English and studied American history at school. The test was not a problem for her.

Lourdes passed the interview and test. The final step was a citizenship ceremony.

At the ceremony, a group of new citizens gathered at a courthouse. With the others, Lourdes promised to be loyal to the United States. She agreed to obey all the laws.

Lourdes was now a U.S. citizen!

As a citizen, Lourdes enjoys many rights. For one thing, Lourdes can now **vote** in **elections**. Voting is how Americans choose leaders in government.

As a **responsible** citizen, Lourdes knows about current events and issues. She votes in city, state, and national elections. By voting, she helps keep democratic values strong.

Lourdes now has a U.S passport. That means she can travel to other countries easily.

U.S. citizens are allowed to apply for government jobs. Lourdes is thinking about becoming a public school teacher. As a citizen, she can do that.

Prove It

What steps did Lourdes take in order to become a citizen? Where did you find your answers?

A Few Famous Immigrants

by Bronia Cieslik

The United States is a nation of immigrants. People from all over the world come here for freedom and opportunity.

Immigrants have helped to build this nation. They have made the United States a better place. Here are the contributions of just a few.

John Muir (1838–1914) was an immigrant from Scotland. He settled in California's Yosemite Valley. He wrote and spoke about the natural beauty of his new home. His writing persuaded Congress to set up the first national parks. Today Muir is called "the father of the national parks."

Elizabeth Blackwell (1821–1910) was born in England. She came to the United States in 1828. She wanted to go to medical school. People told her not to. Blackwell ignored this **advice**. In 1849, she became the first American woman doctor.

Igor Sikorsky (1889–1972) was born in Russia. As a boy, he dreamed of flying machines. Sikorsky moved to the United States in 1919. He invented the first successful helicopter.

Madeleine Albright (born in 1937) left Czechoslovakia in 1948. After college, she worked for the U.S. government. When the United States had problems with other countries, Albright worked to find solutions. In 1997, she became the secretary of state.

301

Community Service Groups

by Angela Diaz

We each live in a community. We all can make our communities better. One way is to become good citizens ourselves.

There are many clubs and groups kids can join. These organizations can help their members and also the community.

4-H

There are over 90,000 4-H clubs in the United States. Members of 4-H learn many skills. They study farming, science, and healthy living. They also learn to be leaders and good citizens.

The 4-H motto is "To make the best better." One way members do that is by serving their communities.

Boy Scouts

Boy Scouts learn to be leaders and good citizens. Since 1910, millions of boys have enjoyed scouting. They have learned useful skills, too. For example, they practice first aid and water rescue. They are prepared for an emergency.

The Boy Scout slogan is "Do a good turn daily." That means helping other people every day. Many scouts complete special service projects. Some clean up parks and streams. Others volunteer in libraries, schools, and food pantries. By being good citizens, they make their communities better.

Girl Scouts

Over 3 million American girls are Girl Scouts. Members have a lot of fun together. Scouting is serious, though. Girl Scouts learn to be strong and confident. They practice doing the right thing. That makes the world a better place.

Part of the Girl Scout promise is "to help other people at all times." Scouts serve in their communities. For example, some run an anti-bullying **campaign** in schools. Others work to end violence in their communities. Taking care of the environment is another goal of Girl Scouts.

Boys & Girls Clubs

Over 4 million young Americans belong to Boys & Girls Clubs. There are over 4,000 of these clubs. They are in all 50 states.

The clubs have many different after-school programs. Members keep fit with sports and games. They work on reading and math skills. An arts program helps develop creative talents. Leadership programs help young people become caring citizens.

Boys & Girls Clubs are a safe place to learn and grow. They're a place where better lives and communities begin.

Zoom In

What are some of the ways that Girl Scouts follow the promise "to help other people at all times"?

305

Earth Force

Many young people want to improve the environment. Earth Force helps them do it. This group teaches young people about the environment. It also shows them how to make it better.

Club members focus on their own community. They find out about the environmental problems there. They choose one to work on. Then they research the issue. Finally, they set a goal for action and go to work!

Members of Earth Force are partners with other community workers. Together they make the environment better for everyone.

Adopt a Highway

Adopting a highway may sound strange. It's very useful, though. Any group or organization can take part. Members of the group pay for the cleanup of part of a road. It's a simple way to make the community cleaner.

In return, the group is allowed to put up a sign along the highway. The sign helps people learn about the group.

Often, groups work to clean up parks or beaches on their own, too.

Prove It

Which group is the most interesting or inspiring? Which details made you choose that group?

The Community Service Library

by Courtney Marks

Community libraries have been around for hundreds of years. Lending books to people was always their purpose. Often, the library was the only place to get a book.

Today the library still lends books. Libraries are changing, though. Here are some of the many things that today's library does.

A Meeting Place

Libraries are community meeting places. Many libraries have special community rooms. People gather there to hold meetings. Experts give talks and advice. There might even be a concert. People also meet to talk about community problems and solutions at the library.

Internet Connections

Many people do not have Internet service at home. Many don't have their own computers. For these people, the library is the place to go. The number of computers in libraries keeps rising. People can use them to write e-mail, do research, or surf the Web.

Learning Centers

Many libraries work to educate people in the community. For young children, there is story time. For older kids, there are arts-and-crafts workshops. For teens, there might be homework help. You can sometimes learn English as a second language at the library. Many libraries help people get ready for the citizenship exam.

Employment Centers

The library is a place to go for job information. The library's many newspapers and computers are places to find "Help Wanted" ads. Libraries also have information about government jobs. Job counselors often volunteer at libraries, too.

Entertainment Centers

You can borrow more than books from your library. Some libraries have DVDs of movies and TV shows. Some have CDs of your favorite music. If you like to listen to stories, there are audiobooks. The library is an entertaining place!

A Special Needs Place

Many people have special needs. Large-print books and audiobooks help those who have trouble seeing.

Some people can't get to the library. Some libraries mail books to them. Library vans travel to out-of-the-way locations. Books in foreign languages are also available.

What else do libraries do? The list goes on and on. If you don't use your library, however, you may never find out.

So visit your local library soon. Walk in, look around, and talk to a librarian. You might just find the help you need!

Prove It

Name two things that the library does to serve the community. Where did you find your answers?

ELECTING OUR LEADERS

by Ellen Ross

Our country is a democracy. That means that people vote for their leaders. Citizens elect the leaders of their nation, state, and community.

The people running for office are called candidates. Candidates run campaigns to get elected. They give **speeches**. They put up signs. They talk to voters and listen to their problems. Sometimes the voters give the candidates advice.

On Election Day, people go to their polling places. A polling place is where citizens vote. Schools are sometimes used as polling places.

After the polling places close, officials count the votes. The candidates with the most votes win.

Electing National Leaders

The President is the leader of the United States. Every four years, citizens vote for a President. The winning candidate serves for four years.

A person can be elected President twice, and serve for eight years in all.

Senators and representatives are national leaders, too. They are elected to the U.S. Congress. There, they pass the laws that govern our country.

Every state has two U.S. senators. Each senator runs for office every six years.

Representatives serve two-year terms in Congress. Then they must run for re-election.

Electing State Leaders

Every state has its own government. A governor heads the state government. A state legislature makes state laws. State courts decide whether the laws are fair.

The citizens of each state elect their state officials. On Election Day, people vote for candidates for state offices.

Most states elect a governor for a four-year term. Members of state legislatures are usually elected either every two years or every four years. Voters also elect some state judges.

Citizens also vote on state issues on Election Day. They may vote for or against raising money to build a new highway, for example.

Electing Local Leaders

Cities and towns have their own governments. Officials of these local governments are elected by the voters.

Many cities elect a mayor. The mayor runs the government of a city. **City council** members are also elected. The city council helps the mayor govern.

Some cities have a city manager, not a mayor. A city manager is not elected. Instead, the city council hires a city manager to run the city.

City governments do important work. They make decisions about city services such as parks, libraries, schools, and police and fire protection.

Prove It

What details support the idea that citizens choose many of the people who serve in their governments?

WHY FRANK PICKING SHOULDN'T WIN

by Rob Domino

I'm angry! I'll tell you why I'm angry. You know Frank Picking? Well, forget Frank Picking. He thinks he should be mayor. Well, he should not. He doesn't deserve to be mayor.

Frank Picking's campaign is a joke. His speeches are all lies. He will say anything you want to hear. Do you want a new park for the city? He will promise you a new park. But he won't keep his promise.

If Frank Picking becomes mayor, there won't be a new park. We'll be lucky if we get to keep the old park. If he's mayor, we'll be lucky if we get to keep anything at all!

If Frank Picking is voted mayor, the city council will be like a circus. It will be like a circus with more clowns than usual.

Some people say that Frank Picking is a responsible man. They are wrong. I went to kindergarten with him. He knocked over my blocks. That's not responsible.

There's another good reason not to vote for Frank Picking. If you vote for him, you can't vote for me. Vote for me! Vote for me!

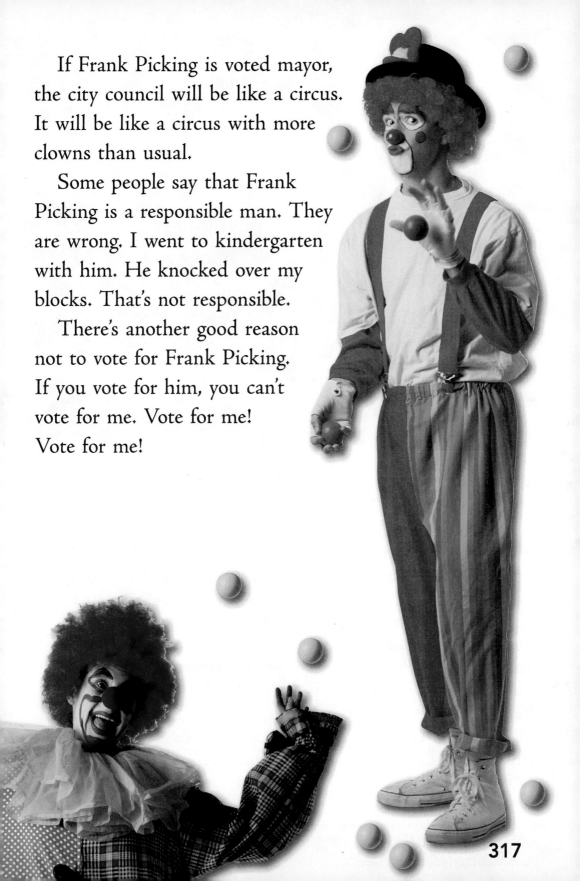

Learn the Words

problem

solution

advice

present

speech

city council

- Read the words on the list.
- Read the dialogue.
- Find the words.

On TV, they said that our community center will be torn down.

That's a big **problem**!

1. You Are the Reporter
Listening and Speaking

You are reporting on a city council meeting. The people in the picture are trying to save the community center. One person gives a speech to the council. Prepare your news story. Tell what happens at the meeting. Give the main points from the speech. Present your news report to the class.

2. Take a Survey
Graphic Organizer

The community center in the picture plans to add one new program. What should it be? Ask a few classmates. Tally their votes. Share your findings with your partner.

Which new program should the community center start?	
an after-school program for kids	
computer classes	
English-language classes	

3. Write an Advice Column
Writing

The community center's newspaper has an advice column. Suppose you are writing it. Work with a partner. Ask three questions. Each should be about an everyday problem. Then write a solution for each problem. Your questions or answers could be funny! Use the advice column in this unit as a model.

4. Make a Speech
Listening and Speaking

Work with your partner. What if you could talk to your city or town council? What problem would you tell them about? Plan a speech. Tell about the problem. If you can think of a solution, tell about it. Ask questions if your partner uses words you don't understand. Give your speech to the class.

Unusual White House Pets

by Carlos Montoya

Every President since 1800 has lived and worked in the White House in Washington, DC. Their families have lived there too. And like most families, they kept pets. Let's look at some unusual White House pets.

Thomas Jefferson (1801) had a pet mockingbird. It sat on his shoulder while he worked at his desk.

The White House was no place for tigers. Martin Van Buren (1837) didn't keep his tiger cubs for very long.

Abraham Lincoln (1861) had two goats. They pulled Lincoln's son in a cart down the White House halls.

Theodore Roosevelt (1901) got a pony for his son. The pony once rode up the White House elevator.

Woodrow Wilson (1913) kept sheep on the White House lawn. It was a good way to mow the grass.

Calvin Coolidge (1923) walked his pet raccoon on a leash. He also had a pet bobcat!

Herbert Hoover (1929) had two pet alligators. They wandered loose around the White House.

From FRANCE, with LOVE

By Mark O'Brien

The Statue of Liberty stands for freedom. One hand holds a bright lamp. The other holds a book of laws. For millions of immigrants, the statue meant freedom. It was the first sight that many of them had of their new country.

The Statue of Liberty was shipped to the United States in 1884. Over 200 huge crates held the pieces. Workers put the statue together on an island in New York Harbor. They built a stone base for the statue.

The Statue of Liberty opened to the public in 1886. Millions of people visit the Statue of Liberty every year. Visitors may climb up inside the statue. There are 354 steps up to the crown.

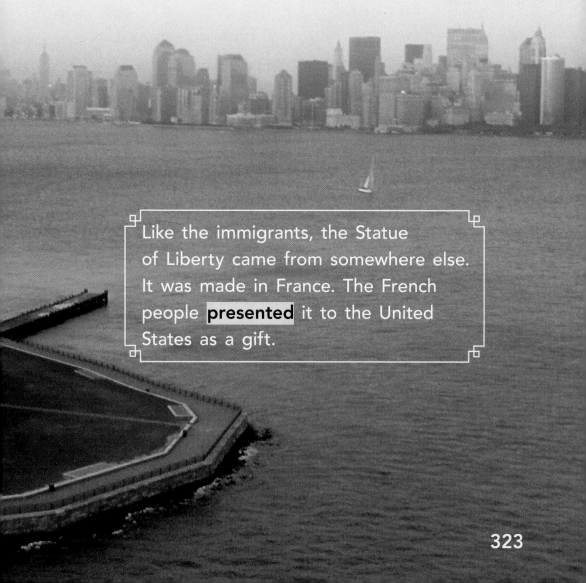

Like the immigrants, the Statue of Liberty came from somewhere else. It was made in France. The French people **presented** it to the United States as a gift.

Retell "Community Service Groups"

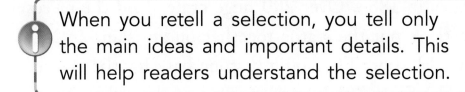

When you retell a selection, you tell only the main ideas and important details. This will help readers understand the selection.

"Community Service Groups" is nonfiction. It gives facts about how people help their communities. Review the selection on pages 302–307. Look at the pictures on page 325.

■ **First and Second Pictures:** How do some clubs give kids a chance to serve the community?

■ **Third Picture:** What club gives kids a safe place for after-school programs?

■ **Fourth and Fifth Pictures:** In what clubs do members work together to help the environment or clean up the community?

Use the pictures on page 325 to retell the selection to your partner. As you tell about each part, point to the correct pictures. Use complete sentences.

Words you might use in your retelling:	
community	citizen
problem	solution

how to help the community

4-H

Boy Scouts
and Girl
Scouts

Boys & Girls
Club

Earth Force

Adopt a
Highway

Dig Deeper

Look Back

Here are some needs of a community.

■ People who cannot see well need large-print books.

■ A highway is full of litter and needs to be cleaned up.

■ Kids need a safe place to go after school.

What group or place can help with each problem? Work with a partner. Look back at this unit. Write down the best group or place for each problem. Put the page number where you found the information. Explain why you and your partner decided on each answer.

Talk About It

Lourdes wants to be an American citizen.

First, she has to live in the United States for five years.

Next, she has to fill out forms.

Then, she has to take a test.

Finally, Lourdes became an American citizen!

In your own words, tell about another series of events or a process. Use words such as *first, next, then,* and *finally.*

Conversation

Talk to a partner. One of you will be person A. The other will be person B.

Person A	Person B

Ask how your partner feels.

Reply. Ask how your partner feels.

Reply. Ask if your partner needs anything.

Reply. Ask what your partner needs.

Reply. Thank your partner.

Thank your partner.

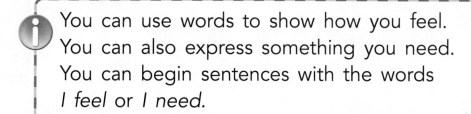

In the MONEY

The **BIG** Question

How do we earn and spend money?

☐ What are some ways that people earn money?

☐ What do people do with the money they earn?

☐ How have forms of money changed from the past until now?

Let's Talk

What is money, and what is it used for?

1. What U.S. coins do you know?

Some U.S. coins are the…

☐ penny.   ☐ nickel.

☐ dime.   ☐ quarter.

2. What could be in a treasure chest?

A treasure chest can hold…

☐ gold.

☐ silver.

☐ gems.

☐ coins and bills.

3. How can you find out the price of something?

You can learn the price by...

☐ asking.

☐ looking at the price tag.

☐ looking it up online.

☐ checking signs in the store.

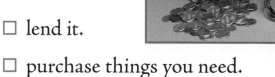

4. What can you do with money?

You can...

☐ save it.

☐ count it.

☐ lend it.

☐ purchase things you need.

Say **more!**

Learn the Words

price
stand
silver
decide
coin
purchase

Theme Vocabulary

The easiest way to remember the meaning of a new word is to use the word. As you discuss money, use these vocabulary words. Use them when you read and write about money, too.

Read the word.
Look at the picture.
Listen to your teacher.

price

stand

silver

decide

coin

purchase

Which Picture?

Look at the vocabulary cards. Choose one picture.
Don't tell anyone what it is! Describe the picture.
See if your partner can guess which picture you chose.

Art Test

Panel 1: Mrs. Hart is out sick. I need you to pick students for her new art class.

Panel 2: But I teach math. I don't know anything about art!

Just give an art test, and pick the best five.

Panel 3: When I was a kid, they said to stay inside the lines. I guess that's the rule.

Panel 4: Okay, class. Your first test is to color this car. Be sure to stay inside the lines.

Panel 5: What do you think, Mr. Stark?

You broke the rules, Darnell. You did not stay inside the lines.

Panel 6: But it looks cool!

I dig it!

Me too!

6) **Formal/Informal Language** "I dig it!" is an informal expression. What do you think it means? How could you say "I dig it!" in a more formal way?

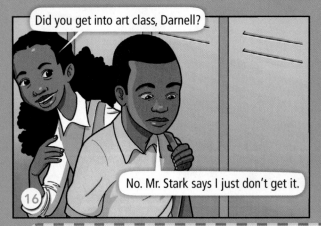

15 **Formal/Informal Language** When you say that someone does not get something, you mean that the person does not understand it. Is this formal or informal language?

20 Formal/Informal Language How could Mr. Stark say "I guess I just don't get art" in a more formal way?

MONEY
IN THE
UNITED STATES

by Angela Castillo

 cent — This **coin** is often called a penny. Pennies have a smooth outer edge.

 nickel — Today Thomas Jefferson appears on the front. Nickels used to show a buffalo and an American Indian.

 dime — The dime has three layers of metal. This coin shows symbols of peace, freedom, and strength.

 quarter — Images and symbols from each of our fifty states appear on many quarters today.

 **half dollar** — John F. Kennedy appears on the front of the half dollar. The American eagle, a symbol of the United States, is on the back.

 dollar — Today's "golden dollar" coins are not really made of gold.

All the paper money in the United States is the same size. A green U.S. Treasury seal appears on all **bills**. But each bill shows a different American leader. For instance, George Washington is on the $1 bill.

Today, many bills contain features to stop people from making fake money. Did you know that some bills have a thread that glows under special lights?

Hundreds of billions of U.S. dollars are in use today. When bills wear out, they are shredded. New bills are printed to replace the old ones.

These are the bills we use most often.

What Would You Do
by Marianna Higgins

What would you do with a million bucks?
I'd go to the park to feed the ducks
the very best food that money can buy
so they'd make a big fuss every time I come by.

What would you do with a wad of cash?
I'd go to the ocean to hear the waves crash.
I'd sit and eat sandwiches fit for a king
with mustard and pickles and everything.

with a Million Bucks?

What would you do with a pile of money?
I'd buy myself a real live bunny
and maybe and a dog and a Siamese cat
who'd sleep in my room on a Turkish mat.

What would you do with a pot of gold?
I'd go to a store where the best books are sold.
I'd buy up everything they had in the place
and read each one at my very own pace.

Cool Jobs in an Animated World

by Carla Alvarez

For most people, a cool job means doing something they love. An artistic person who loves movies might become an animator. Animators are known for drawing great characters. Actors enjoy using their voices to bring animated characters to life. Today, some cool new jobs have opened up in the world of film for both artists and actors.

The process starts when an actor puts on a special suit with sensors on it. Cameras pick up everything the actor does. It may be a slight smile or a giant leap. The data from the sensors then goes to a computer. The process is called motion-capture acting.

The next step involves the animator. She makes use of both her artistic and computer skills. Step by step, she places the motion-capture actor's movements into a visual shell she has created. This outer shell can look like anything the animator wants. It may be an animal, an alien, or a human of any size and shape.

Characters created this way are becoming more popular in sci-fi movies and in computer games. That means the number of cool jobs for skilled actors and animators is greater than ever.

Build Your Own Budget

by Eva Anderson

Young people everywhere look forward to the time when they "make it" on their own. That means having a job, an apartment, and money to live on. But doing well on one's own takes some planning. That's where a budget comes in handy. It can help people to manage the money they have.

The first step in making a budget is writing down one's income. This is how much a person earns each month. The second step is figuring out one's expenses. Expenses are the things that a person spends his or her money on each month.

When people live on their own, they have expenses. For one, they must pay for housing. That may mean apartment rent. Or it may mean a house payment. Usually the cost of gas and electricity is extra. Food is another common expense. It includes groceries and the amount spent in restaurants. Another expense is transport, such as bus and subway fares. It might include costs to take care of a car. Other common expenses include health care and personal care. There is also entertainment, the fun things a person pays for each month. Movies are a good example.

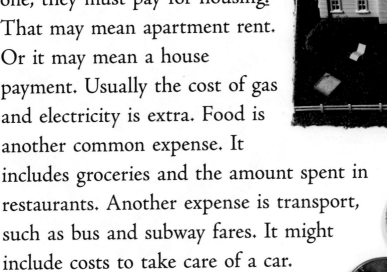

One's expenses should not be greater than one's income. Think of that income as a whole pie, and each expense as a piece of the pie. Typically, housing costs use up about one fourth to one third of the pie. Food costs are less than that. Many former students must add another piece to their pie: paying back student loans.

Of course, not everyone will have the same-size pie pieces. For instance, the **price** of food and rent in big cities is often higher than in small towns. People who walk to work will pay less for transport. That will give them more to spend elsewhere.

Sometimes people spend more than they earn. When that happens, they must **decide** where to cut back on expenses. Does that mean going out to eat less? Does it mean buying fewer clothes? A budget can help a person figure out the best action to take.

People should also plan to save some money. A budget can help someone save a little each month. This piece of the pie would be left alone to grow over time. It's like a hidden **treasure** waiting to be used when needed.

Prove It

Which paragraph explains what expenses are?

347

MONEY
THROUGH THE AGES

by Joanna Fielding

In prehistoric times, people didn't use money. They simply traded items with other members of their clan. They had many items to trade. Some members were good at gathering certain plants. Other members were good hunters. Everyone had need for items they couldn't easily get on their own.

About ten thousand years ago, more and more families began to settle in the same place. They became farmers. Their communities grew. This made the simple trading of items more difficult. As a result, people began to use certain objects as a form of money. These items had to have a value that everyone agreed on.

These ancient farmers often used grain as money. They chose grain because the community members agreed it had value. But how much was it worth? The community worked together to figure that out. Once they agreed on an amount, people in some places began using grain whenever they wanted to trade for the things they needed.

Grain wasn't the only object that people used as money. Thousands of years ago in China and parts of Africa, shells and salt were used as money. In other places, cattle was a form of money.

Zoom In

Why did people trade items with each other in prehistoric times? Where did you find your answer?

In the United States, American Indian tribes once used beads made from shells as money. Farther south in Mexico, early tribes used cacao beans. Cacao is the main ingredient in chocolate. Unfortunately, this prized food led people driven by **greed** to replace the core of the beans with mud. As a result, tribe members didn't know which cacao bean was real and which was not.

Making false money was not limited to cacao beans, though. In other parts of the world, money made from valuable metals had this same problem. To solve this problem, some ancient peoples hired an expert. He decided if the money was good. If so, he placed his mark on it.

In time, governments put their own stamp on small pieces of metal money. These were the first coins. They were created about 2,500 years ago in areas of Turkey and China. It didn't take long before coins were used in other countries, too. In Europe and India, they used **silver** and gold. Coins in regions around China were often made of copper and brass. The shapes and designs of coins were different. But all coins were made by hand.

Unlike early coins, modern coins are made by machine. Also, modern coins are actually worth more than the metal used to create them!

The first use of paper money was in China in the seventh century A.D. People liked it because it was easy to carry around. Its name was *fei qian*, which means "flying money."

About a thousand years later, European governments started using paper money to represent gold coins. Although the paper had little value in itself, a person could still trade it in for gold.

During the twentieth century, most governments ended paper money's ties to gold. In other words, banks would no longer give a person gold for his paper money. Even so, people are still using paper money to pay for goods and services.

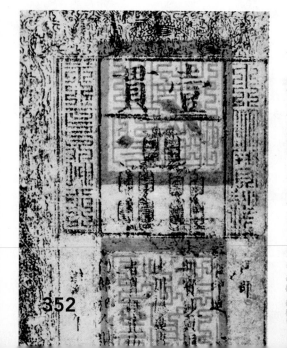

Starting in the late 1900s, electronic forms of money began to replace paper money and coins. Today, people use credit and debit cards to **purchase** items all the time. Also, someone with a bank account can receive automatic payments from others, and make payments, without having to use actual money. In fact, some people carry very few coins and bills around with them.

Do consumers pay a price for this? Usually they don't, because the process saves banks time and money, too.

Prove It

What are some of the ways money has changed over time? Where did you find your answers?

Money: The Same But Different

by Matthew Sloan

All over the world, people use bills and coins to pay for goods and services. Americans purchase things using dollars and cents. The basic unit of money in the United States is the U.S. dollar. The Canadian dollar is the unit of money in Canada. In Australia, people use the Australian dollar. Other countries across the globe use different units of money. The peso, for instance, is used in Mexico. In China, the yuan is used. In much of Europe, the euro is the unit of money. Other units around the world include the ruble, pound, dinar, and rupee.

Just as money has different names, the way it looks changes from country to country. Take printed bills, for example. Their colors and sizes are not the same around the world. There is also a difference in who and what might appear on printed bills. Every nation wants to salute its own great people and places.

Many countries show their heads of state on printed money. The United States shows past Presidents. Some nations honor their kings and queens. In Egypt, ancient Queen Nefertiti has appeared on several bills. In England, Queen Elizabeth II appears on printed money and on coins.

In some countries, great people in the arts are honored. In Denmark, for instance, the author Hans Christian Andersen has been given a place on a paper bill. Danish painters and poets have also received this honor.

Elsewhere, business leaders and inventors are shown on printed money. So are scientists and engineers. In Northern Ireland, for example, John Boyd Dunlop was honored in this way. He founded an important tire company.

Every year, there are new leaders, artists, scientists, and business people all over the world. As their fame increases, so does the desire to salute them in some way. But it's **foolish** to think that every great person will appear on printed money. That is saved for those who have won a special place in a nation's heart.

Around the world, people use these bills every day. They buy sandwiches, bikes, and clothes. They pay for haircuts and doctor visits. Paper money is part of daily life all across the globe.

Prove It

Who are some of the people who have been honored on paper money around the world? Where did you find your answers?

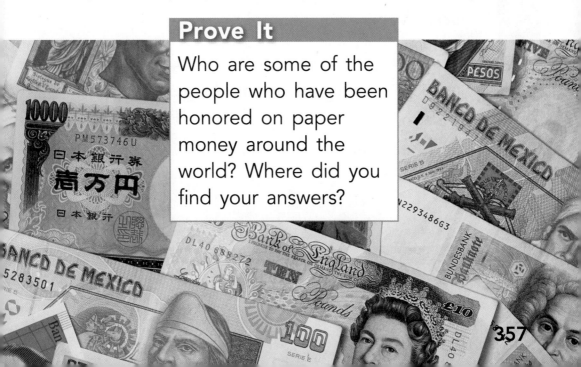

THE JOB FAIR

by Susan M. Meredith

CAST OF CHARACTERS
MARIA, TV interviewer
MILO, student
HEATHER, student
MR. FRASER, employer
MS. KLINE, employer
RUSSELL, student

Setting: Friday morning in a college gym. MARIA is doing a TV news story about the job fair.

MARIA: *(faces the turned-on camera and smiles)* We're here at the job fair. It brings employers and student job seekers together. (MILO enters.) What's your name?

MILO: Milo. I'm a student here. I'm hoping to get a job after I graduate. I'll be going from booth to booth to introduce myself and pass out my resumé.

MARIA: What are some jobs you've had?

MILO: Well, these days I'm working part-time in a science lab. But during high school I shoveled snow in the winter, and I had a lemonade **stand** when I was young.

MARIA: What kind of work are you looking for?

MILO: A job in science. I want to do stuff that really interests me, not just one that gives me a big salary. I don't need fame or **fortune**.

MILO: (*seeing a friend walking by*) Hi, Heather.

HEATHER: Oh, hi, Milo. (*suddenly noticing she's on-camera*)

MARIA: So, Heather, what's your game plan?

Zoom In

What jobs has Milo had before?

HEATHER: Well, I'm here to check out possible employers. I visited some of their websites during the last few days.

MARIA: Do you think employers are here to check out the job seekers, too?

HEATHER: Absolutely. That's why I have a pitch all ready to go. It is a quick summary of my skills and experience. I hope it will grab their attention.

MARIA: I hope it does. Have fun! (*As the two students leave,* MARIA *walks toward* MR. FRASER.) Now let's chat with some employers to see what they're looking for. Here's one now.

MARIA: Good morning, sir. How do you choose among job seekers?

MR. FRASER: A good résumé is important, of course. But our company is looking for someone who is confident. We want to feel that our new employee can solve problems that come up. I also want them to ask questions, to take notes, to pay attention.

MARIA: (*A student job seeker walks up to* MR. FRASER's *booth.*) Well, let me give you a chance to meet and greet this student. (MARIA *walks to another booth.*) Hi, have you met any job seekers today that are right for your company?

MS. KLINE: Yes, several. And it's not even noon yet!

MARIA: Tell me what makes a person "right" for you. You have a retail store in town?

MS. KLINE: I do. Our employees need to be friendly and polite.

MARIA: So it probably wouldn't be wise to come to your booth dressed in old jeans.

MS. KLINE: That would be foolish, especially if they want to impress me.

MARIA: Thank you for sharing your thoughts with us. Here's Heather again. (*Walking along, she sees* HEATHER *talking with* RUSSELL.) How is your day going?

HEATHER: I've had some great meetings already. My friend Russell here has also had a good morning.

RUSSELL: I went to a workshop on résumé writing and met with people from several companies.

HEATHER: Later on, we're both going to send thank-you e-mails to the employers we've met.

MARIA: Do either of you have any advice?

RUSSELL: Meet as many people as you can and learn as much as you can.

MARIA: (*to camera*) Wise words from two job seekers. I'm Maria Sanchez at the job fair.

THE END

Prove It

Use details from the play to explain which job-seeking information is the most useful.

Learn the Words

fortune
increase
treasure
bill
foolish
greed

- Read the words on the list.
- Read the dialogue.
- Find the words.

(speech bubble in image): There's still silver in these mines. Maybe we'll have good **fortune** and find some!

1. Finding Treasure
Writing

Suppose you are at the mine in the picture. You have found some silver! What did you do with your treasure? Write about two things you did. Explain why you did these things. Use earlier first-person selections from this book if you need a model for writing in first person.

2. Make a Venn Diagram
Graphic Organizer

Bills and coins are two kinds of money. Think about what each kind is like. Fill each oval in the Venn diagram with details. Share your diagram with your partner.

Bills and Coins

bills | both | coins

3. You Are the Actor
Listening and Speaking

Work with a partner. Take turns reading the dialogue in the picture. First, ask your partner about any words you don't understand. Use your best acting voice when you read. Make the dialogue come alive.

4. What Is Greedy?
Writing

Come up with an action that shows greed. It can be something that one person does. It can be something that a group does. Tell about the action in a paragraph. Explain why this action shows greed. Exchange paragraphs with a partner. Ask your partner about any words you don't understand.

Treasure Lost . . . and Found

By Charles Warren

For centuries, ships have crossed the seas carrying valuable goods. In the past, these riches included gold or silver, often in the form of coins. Precious jewels and statues were sometimes on board as well.

But there are many stories about ships that never reached port. Why didn't they get to their destination? Some vessels sank at sea for unknown reasons. Perhaps there was a fierce storm. But other ships may have been too damaged by pirates to carry on. Of course, even pirate ships sank in the ocean at times. The stolen goods on board went down with the ship.

Today, lost treasure worth millions still rests among the remains of these sunken ships. But where are the wrecks? Studying history has given treasure hunters some clues:

- During ancient times, vessels often carried riches across the Mediterranean Sea. Many of these ships disappeared.
- In the 1600s, many ships loaded with jewels and ivory sank in the Indian Ocean.
- Between 1500 and the early 1800s, the Caribbean Sea claimed a large number of Spanish ships carrying riches.

In some of these cases, greedy pirates may have taken the riches and destroyed the ships.

Seeking their own fortunes, treasure hunters have tried to find sunken ships. But finding a ship's remains rarely happens by accident.

To get started, most treasure hunters study old newspapers and logbooks. After months of research, these hunters head for the sea. There, they use high-tech equipment to locate the wreck. The process is hard, though. The remains are often covered in mud, sand, or even coral. But the hunters, wearing scuba gear, dive in. If all goes well, they find the remains. Then it takes months of careful work to bring up the sunken treasure.

But who is the owner of the sunken treasure? The ship's remains may be the property of the government that first sent the vessel to sea. Or a particular company may own a ship, even one from the past.

Laws are in place to figure out who owns the ship. Of course, sometimes no one has that answer. In such a case the treasure hunter might be able to keep what he or she finds.

Some treasure hunters have a contract with the owner. It states that the hunter gets paid when he or she finds the wreck. Hunters who bring back more riches often earn more.

Prove It

How do treasure hunters know where to look for treasure? Where did you find your answer?

Retell "Money Through the Ages"

> To retell a selection, give the most important points and details. Some selections present details in time order. Use words such as *before* or *later* to make your meaning clear.

"Money Through the Ages" is a nonfiction article. It gives facts about forms of money. Review the selection on pages 348–353. Look at the chart on page 371.

- Before 2,500 years ago: What items were used as money? Why?

- About 2,500 years ago: Where were the first coins used? How were they different from earlier forms of money?

- About 1,300 years ago: What new form of money was used at this time? How was it different from earlier forms of money?

Use the pictures on page 371 to retell the selection to your partner. As you tell about each form of money, point to the correct picture. Use complete sentences.

Words you might use in your retelling:	
price	silver
coin	bill

Before 2,500 years ago

About 2,500 years ago

About 1,300 years ago

Dig Deeper

Look Back

Find three selections in this unit that give facts about coins and bills. One of them tells *mainly* about how different countries have different kinds of coins and bills. On your paper, answer these questions.

1. What is the title of the selection that tells about money around the world?

2. What details let you know that this selection tells mainly about money around the world? Give at least two details.

3. How are the other selections about coins and bills different from this one?

Talk About It

What would you use as money instead of the coins and bills we use now?

Why did you choose that item?

What did your classmates choose?

Do you agree? Why or why not?

If not, how could you convince others to change their minds? How could someone else convince you?

Conversation

 It's fun to discuss what you like and dislike. Use words, but show your feelings in your face, too. Remember—be polite if you disagree with someone else.

Talk to a partner. One of you will be person A. The other will be person B.

Person A   **Person B**

Tell about something you like.

                         Agree or disagree. Then tell about something you like.

Agree or disagree. Then tell about something you dislike.

                         Agree or disagree. Tell about something you dislike.

Agree or disagree. Ask about something else your partner likes.

                         Answer your partner.

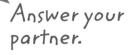

GLOSSARY

advanced

A

ad·vanced (ăd-vănst′) *adj.* greatly developed, using new ideas

ad·vice (ăd-vīs′) *n.* what other people tell you to help you solve a problem

af·fect (ə-fĕkt′) *tr.v.* to make a difference to something

as·sem·bly line (ə-sĕm′blē) (līn) *n.* a part of a factory where work passes from one person or machine to the next

as·tro·naut (ăs′trə-nôt′) *n.* someone who travels and works in space

B

bill (bĭl) *n.* the mouth of a bird

bill (bĭl) *n.* a piece of paper money

bird (bûrd) *n.* an animal that has wings and feathers

bill

ă pat / ā pay / âr care / ä father / ĕ pet / ē bee /
ĭ pit / ī pie / îr pier / ŏ pot / ō toe / ô paw /

374 Glossary

C

cal·cu·la·tor (kăl′kyə-lā′tər) *n.* a machine that helps find answers to math problems

cam·paign (kăm-pān′) *n.* the planned activities a person does to try to win an election

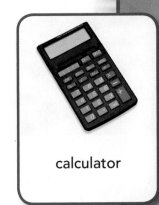

calculator

care·less (kâr′lĭs) *adj.* without attention or thought to avoid mistakes or harm

cause (kôz) *v.* to make something happen

cel·e·brate (sĕl′ə-brāt′) *v.* to do things for a special event or day

cen·tu·ry (sĕn′chə-rē) *n.* one hundred years

chemical (kĕm′ ĭ-kəl) *n.* a liquid or other kind of material made by people

chore (chôr) *n.* a job that has to be done often

cit·i·zen (sĭt′ĭ-zən) *n.* a person who lives in a certain city, state, or country

citizen

oi **noise** / ŏŏ **took** / ōō **boot** / ou **out** / ŭ **cut** / ûr **firm** / hw **which** /
th **thin** / *th* **this** / zh **vision** / ə **about, item, edible, gallop, circus**

coin

cit·y coun·cil (sĭt'ē) (koun'səl) *n.* a group of people who work together to lead their community and make decisions

coin (koin) *n.* a small piece of metal that is worth a certain amount and is used as money

com·mand (kə-mănd') *n.* an order to do something

com·mon (kŏm'ən) *adj.* appearing often or many times

com·mu·ni·ty (kə-myōō'nĭ-tē) *n.* a group of people who live in the same area or who do things together

com·pass rose (kŭm'pəs) (rōz) *n.* a circle on a map showing the directions north, south, east, and west

com·put·er (kəm-pyōō'tər) *n.* a machine that people use to to find information, play games, and do work

conserve

con·serve (kən-sûrv') *v.* to try to save something

con·ti·nent (kŏn'tə-nənt) *n.* one of the seven large, main land areas of the world

creek (krēk, krĭk) *n.* a small stream of water

ă pat / ā pay / âr care / ä father / ĕ pet / ē bee /
ĭ pit / ī pie / îr pier / ŏ pot / ō toe / ô paw /

crew (krōō) *n.* a team of people who work together to do a job

D

dec·ade (dĕk′ād′) *n.* ten years

de·cide (dĭ-sīd′) *v.* to think about something and make a choice

de·scribe (dĭ-skrīb′) *tr.v.* to use words to tell what something is like

E

e·lec·tion (ĭ-lĕk′shən) *n.* an event where people choose leaders or decide something by voting

e·lec·tric·i·ty (ĭ-lĕk-trĭs′ĭ-tē) *n.* energy, or power, that travels along wires

en·er·gy (ĕn′ər-jē) *n.* power that makes machines work

ex·pe·ri·ence (ĭk-spîr′ē-əns) *v.* to take part in an event

F

farm·ing (färm′ing) *v.* growing crops or raising animals

electricity

farming

oi noise / ŏŏ took / ōō boot / ou out / ŭ cut / ûr firm / hw which /
th thin / *th* this / zh vision / ə about, item, edible, gallop, circus

377

fish

fin (fĭn) *n.* the body part of a fish that helps it swim in different directions

fish (fĭsh) *n.* an animal that lives in the water and has gills and fins

fish·ing (fĭsh′ing) *v.* to catch fish or other animals that live in the water

fool·ish (foo′lĭsh) *adj.* unwise and lacking good sense

for·tune (fôr′chən) *n.* luck

G

gal·lon (găl′ən) *n.* a liquid measure that equals four quarts, or thirty-two cups

gar·bage (gär′bĭj) *n.* things that are no longer needed or wanted

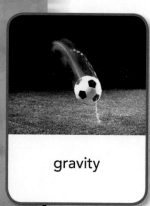
gravity

grav·i·ty (grăv′ĭ-tē) *n.* the force that pulls an object down to the surface of Earth

greed (grēd) *n.* the desire for more money or things than a person needs

H

harm (härm) *v.* to hurt

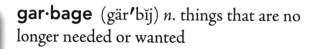
ă pat / ā pay / âr care / ä father / ĕ pet / ē bee /
ĭ pit / ī pie / îr pier / ŏ pot / ō toe / ô paw /

I

in·crease (ĭn-krēs′) *v.* to get bigger or to go higher

K

key·board (kē′bôrd′) *n.* the set of lettered and numbered keys used with a computer

M

mam·mal (măm′əl) *n.* an animal that feeds its young with milk

mar·ket (mär′kĭt) *n.* a place where people buy and sell things

mod·ern (mŏd′ərn) *adj.* new and from the present

mon·i·tor (mŏn′ĭ-tər) *n.* the part of a computer that shows words and pictures

market

N

nat·u·ral re·sourc·es (năch′ər-əl) (rē′sôrs′əz) *n.pl.* things found in nature that are very useful to us

na·ture (nā′chər) *n.* everything in the world that is not made by people

nature

oi **noise** / ŏŏ **took** / ōō **boot** / ou **out** / ŭ **cut** / ûr **firm** / hw **which** / th **thin** / *th* **this** / zh **vision** / ə **about, item, edible, gallop, circus**

O

oil (oil) *n.* a liquid found deep in the ground that is used for fuel

orbit

or·bit (ôr′bĭt) *v.* to move around the Sun or a planet in a circle

out·er space (ou′tər) (spās) *n.* the huge area far away from Earth

P

past (păst) *n.* a time that has already happened, possibly long ago

phase (fāz) *n.* the shape of the Moon as we see it from Earth

plan (plăn) *n.* a drawing that shows how something is put together

pollute

plan·et (plăn′ĭt) *n.* a large object that moves around the Sun

pol·lute (pə-lo͞ot′) *tr.v.* to make something dirty, or unclean

pop·u·la·tion (pŏp′yə-lā′shən) *n.* the number of people who live in a place

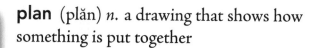

ă pat / ā pay / âr care / ä father / ĕ pet / ē bee /
ĭ pit / ī pie / îr pier / ŏ pot / ō toe / ô paw /

pos·si·ble (pŏs′ə-bəl) *adj.* able to happen or be done

pres·ent (prĕz′ənt) *n.* the period of time that is happening now

pres·ent (prĭ-zĕnt′) *v.* to show or talk about something in front of others

present

price (prīs) *n.* the amount of money that something costs

print·er (prĭn′tər) *n.* a machine that prints words and pictures on paper

prob·lem (prŏb′ləm) *n.* something that causes trouble or needs to be figured out

pur·chase (pûr′chĭs) *tr.v.* to buy

pur·pose (pûr′pəs) *n.* the way something is used

recycle

R

rail·road (rāl′rōd′) *n.* a path of steel tracks on which trains move along

re·cy·cle (rē-sī′kəl) *tr.v.* to treat things that have been used so that they can be used again

oi noise / o͝o took / o͞o boot / ou out / ŭ cut / ûr firm / hw which / th thin / *th* this / zh vision / ə about, item, edible, gallop, circus

re·port (rǐ-pôrt′) *n.* written facts and ideas about a topic

rep·tile (rĕp′tīl′) *n.* an animal that lays eggs and has skin covered with scales

re·spon·si·ble (rǐ-spŏn′sə-bəl) *adj.* trusted to do the right thing

ro·bot (rō′bŏt′) *n.* a machine that can help people do their work

robot

S

scale (skāl) *n.* a feature on a map that helps tell how far apart two places are

scales (skāls) *n.* thin plates that cover and protect the bodies of fish and reptiles

sil·ver (sĭl′vər) *n.* a shiny gray metal that is used to make jewelry, coins, silverware, and other items

so·lar sys·tem (sō′lər) (sĭs′təm) *n.* the Sun, planets, moons, and other objects in space

so·lu·tion (sə-loo′shən) *n.* the answer to a problem

scales

ă pat / ā pay / âr care / ä father / ĕ pet / ē bee /
ĭ pit / ī pie / îr pier / ŏ pot / ō toe / ô paw /

space shut·tle (spās) (shŭt′l) *n.* a spacecraft that can make more than one trip into space

speech (spēch) *n.* thoughts and ideas that are said aloud in a formal way to a group of people

stand (stănd) *n.* a small store

sym·bol (sĭm′bəl) *n.* something that stands for something else

space shuttle

T

trail (trāl) *n.* a path that people can follow

train (trān) *v.* to practice something so you can get better at doing it

trait (trāt) *n.* something that makes one person or animal different from another

trans·por·ta·tion (trăns′pər-tā′shən) *n.* the ways people and things move from one place to another

trail

trav·el (trăv′əl) *v.* to go from one place to another

treas·ure (trĕzh′ər) *n.* a collection of things that are valuable

oi **noise** / o͝o **took** / o͞o **boot** / ou **out** / ŭ **cut** / ûr **firm** / hw **which** /
th **thin** / *th* **this** / zh **vision** / ə **about, item, edible, gallop, circus**

type (tīp) *v.* to write using a computer or typewriter

U

u·nique (yōō-nēk′) *adj.* special, and unlike anything else

V

vote

vote (vōt) *v.* to make a choice

W

weight·less (wāt′lĭs) *adj.* without the pull of gravity

weightless

ă pat / ā pay / âr care / ä father / ĕ pet / ē bee /
ĭ pit / ī pie / îr pier / ŏ pot / ō toe / ô paw /

Acknowledgments

Text Acknowledgments: "The Moondust Footprint" from *We the People: Poems* by Bobbi Katz. Text copyright © 1998, 2000 by Bobbi Katz. Reprinted by permission of HarperCollins Publishers.

Illustration Credits: Nicole Wong, Escletxa

Photography Credits: v (tr) NASA; v © ImageClub/Getty Images; vi (bl) Comstock/Getty Images; vi © Brand X Pictures/Getty Images; vi © Artville / Getty Images; vii Getty Images; vii (t) Corbis; vii PhotoDisc/Getty Images; viii © John Dakers/Life File/PhotoDisc/Getty Images; 2 Photodisc/Getty Images; 2 ©Artville/ Getty Royalty Free; 2 (bl) © Digital Vision / Getty Images; 2 ©Stockbyte/Getty Images; 2 Image Source/Jupiterimages/Getty Images; 3 (b) ©Corbis; 3 (br) © Brand X Pictures/Getty Images; 3 © Stockbyte/Getty Images; 4 © Royalty Free/ CORBIS; 4 (tr) ©Photodisc/Getty Images; 4 (b) ©Getty Images; 5 (br) ©Photodisc/Getty Images; 5 (tr) ©Wim Wiskerke/Alamy Images; 5 © PhotoDisc / Getty Images; 6 © Getty Images RF; 6 (cr) © Getty Images Royalty Free; 7 Corbis; 8 © Photodisc/Getty Images; 8 © Corbis Royalty Free; 8 ©Corbis Royalty Free; 8 (tr) Brand X Pictures/ Getty Images; 8 (bc) ©Corbis; 9 (tr) © Comstock Royalty Free; 9 (tl) Corbis; 16 ©Daniel Grill/Alamy Images; 16 ©Artville/ Getty Royalty Free; 16 Corbis; 16 ©PhotoDisc/gettyimages; 16 Artville/Getty Images; 17 ©Corbis; 17 ©Corbis; 17 Photodisc/Getty Images; 17 Getty Images; 17 (tr) Steve Hamblin / Alamy; 17 (br) © Jules Frazier/ Photodisc/Getty Images; 18 (cl) ©Photodisc/Getty Images; 18 (tl) Photos.com/Jupiterimages/Getty Images; 18 (bl) ©rangizzz/Shutterstock; 18 (bg) © Digital Vision / Getty Images; 19 (br) Stockdisc/Getty Images; 19 (tr) ©Thomas Shjarback/Alamy; 19 (l) © Jack Lewis/TxDOT; 20 ©Houghton Mifflin Harcourt; 20 ©Houghton Mifflin Harcourt; 20 © Corbis Royalty Free; 21 Corbis; 21 Library of Congress; 21 Vintage Classics / Alamy; 26 © Getty Images Royalty Free; 26 (b) © Ernesto Rios Lanz/Sexto Sol/PhotoDisc/Getty Images; 27 © Artville / Getty Images; 28 © Amos Morgan/PhotoDisc/Getty Images; 30 (b) © John Dakers/Life File/PhotoDisc/Getty Images; 31 (tr) Lawrence Manning/Corbis; 32 ©Corbis; 33 © Artville / Getty Images; 46 (br) ©Punchstock/Getty Images; 46 ©Organics image Library/Alamy Images; 49 ©Corbis; 49 (c) © Amos Morgan/PhotoDisc/Getty Images; 49 (bl) © Artville / Getty Images; 49 (tc) © Getty Images Royalty Free; 49 (tl) © Ernesto Rios Lanz/Sexto Sol/PhotoDisc/Getty Images; 49 (cl) © John Dakers/Life File/PhotoDisc/Getty Images; 52 (b) ©Mark Conlin/Getty Images; 52 (cr) © Digital Vision / Getty Images; 52 (br) Photodisc/Getty Images; 52 ©Alamy Images; 54 © DAJ/Getty Images; 54 (bl) ©Comstock/ Getty Images; 54 Digital Vision / Alamy; 54 (br) © Brand X Pictures/Getty Images; 54 (cr) Getty Images/Photodisc; 54 ©Imagebroker/Alamy; 55 (br) © Artville/Getty Images; 55 ©Juniors Bildarchiv/Alamy; 55 (bl) ©PhotoDisc/Getty Images; 55 (t) ©Corbis; 62 (cl) ©Stockbyte/Getty Images; 62 (bl) © Digital Vision / Getty Images; 62 ©Corbis; 63 (tr) © Digital Vision/Getty Images; 63 (br) ©Stockbyte/Getty Images; 63 (cr) Getty Images/Photodisc; 64 (br) ©PhotoDisc/ Getty Royalty Free; 64 (br) ©Radius Images/Getty Images; 64 (bl) ©Kuzmin Andrey/Shutterstock; 64 (tl) Artville/Getty Images; 64 (bl) ©rangizzz/Shutterstock; 65 (tl) ©Artville/Getty Images; 65 (tr) ©Digital Vision/ Getty Images; 65 (br) Stockbyte/Getty Images; 65 (br) © Getty Images; 65 (br) Comstock/Getty Images; 66 ©Photodisc/ Getty Images Royalty Free; 72 Digital Vision / Getty Images; 74 (cr) Don Farrall/Photodisc/Getty Images; 74 (tr) © Dynamic Graphics/Jupiterimages; 74 ©F. Schussler/PhotoLink/Photodisc/Getty Images; 75 ©Getty Images; 76 © Corbis Royalty Free; 77 Gallo Images-Anthony Bannister/Digital Vision/Getty Images; 78 ©foryouinf/Shutterstock; 79 (b) ©Mark Conlin/Getty Images; 80 (b) ©Lynda Richardson/Corbis; 80 (inset) ©Corbis; 81 ©Houghton Mifflin Harcourt; 91 Image Source/Jupiterimages/Getty Images; 91 ©Stockbyte/Getty Images; 92 (t) Stockbyte / Getty Images; 92 (b) ©PhotoLink/Getty Images; 92 (bc) ©searagen/Alamy Images; 92 (bl) Digital Vision/Getty Images; 93 ©Comstock/Getty Images; 93 (tr) ©F Schussler/ PhotoDisc/Getty Images; 93 © Digital Vision/Getty Images; 93 (br) Photodisc/Getty Images; 95 (c) ©Getty Images; 95 (cl) Digital Vision / Getty Images; 95 (bl) © Comstock/Getty Images; 95 (cr) Digital Vision/Getty Images; 95 (cr) Don Farrall/Photodisc/Getty Images; 98 (bl) © Jupiterimages/Brand X/Alamy Ltd; 98 ©Alamy Images; 98 (b) ©Alamy Images; 99 ©Reed Kaestner/ Corbis; 100 (c) ©Cn Boon/Alamy Images; 100 (b) Dynamic Graphics / Getty Images; 101 ©Getty Images; 101 Royalty-Free/Corbis; 101 (b) © Corbis Royalty Free; 101 Photodisc/Getty Images; 108 (cr) © Digital Vision/Getty Images; 109 (tr) © Corbis Royalty Free; 109 (tl) ©Getty Images; 109 (tc) © Stockbyte/Getty Images; 110 (bl) ©rangizzz/Shutterstock; 110 (tl) ©Corbis; 110 (cl) Photodisc/Getty Images; 110 (bl) ©Comstock/Getty Images; 111 (tr) ©Corbis; 112 © Stockbyte/Getty Images; 114 (b) ©Jupiterimages; 114 (cr) ©Corbis; 115 (b) ©Digital Archive Japan/Alamy Images; 116 © Getty Images; 116 (b) From the Collections of The Henry Ford; 117 (b) ©Alamy Images; 127 (b) ©Corbis; 128 (c) Dynamic Graphics / Getty Images; 129 (c) ©Getty Images; 130 (c) Dynamic Graphics / Getty Images; 132 (l) ©NASA; 137 (cr) © Shirley V Beckes/PhotoDisc/Getty Images; 138 (tl) ©panbazil/ Shutterstock; 138 (c) Artville/Getty Images; 138 (tr) NASA; 138 (br) NASA; 138 (b) ©Photodisc/Getty Images; 138 (bl) © Jupiterimages/Brand X/Alamy Ltd; 141 (cr) Comstock/Getty Images; 141 (cl) ©Photodisc/Getty Images; 141 (t) ©Photodisc/Getty Images; 143 (br) © Comstock/Getty Images; 144 (br) ©Comstock/Getty Images; 144 ©Getty Images; 144 © ImageClub/Getty Images; 146 © Siede Preis/PhotoDisc/Getty Images; 146 © PhotoDisc/Getty Images; 146 ©Photodisc/Getty Images; 146 (t) © C Squared Studios/PhotoDisc/Getty Images; 146 PhotoDisc/ Getty Images; 147 (tc) © Brand X Pictures/Getty Images; 147 (tr) © Getty Images; 147 © PhotoDisc/Getty Images; 157 (cr) ©Creatas/Getty Images; 157 (bl) ©Creatas/Getty Images; 157 (br) ©Stockbyte/Getty Images; 158 ©